Storage

Austria

Austria

BY R. CONRAD STEIN

Enchantment of the World
Second Series

Children's Press®

A Division of Grolier Publishing

NEW YORK   LONDON   HONG KONG   SYDNEY
DANBURY, CONNECTICUT

Frontispiece: Cross-country skiing in Tyrol

Consultant: Richard L. Rudolph, Ph.D., Professor of History, University of Minnesota

Please note: All statistics are as up-to-date as possible at the time of publication.

Visit Children's Press on the Internet: http://publishing.grolier.com

Book Production by Herman Adler Design Group

Library of Congress Cataloging-in-Publication Data

Stein, R. Conrad
    Austria / by R. Conrad Stein.
      p. cm. — (Enchantment of the world. Second series)
    Includes bibliographical references and index.
    Summary: Describes the geography, history, plants and animals,
economy, language, religions, culture, and people of Austria.
    ISBN 0-516-21049-1
    1. Austria Juvenile literature. [1. Austria.] I. Title.
II. Series.
DB17.S68 2000
943.6—dc21
                                          99-37401
                                            CIP

Austria

Cover photo:
Hochosterwitz
Castle in Carinthia

Contents

The Spanish Riding School in Vienna

A traditional costume

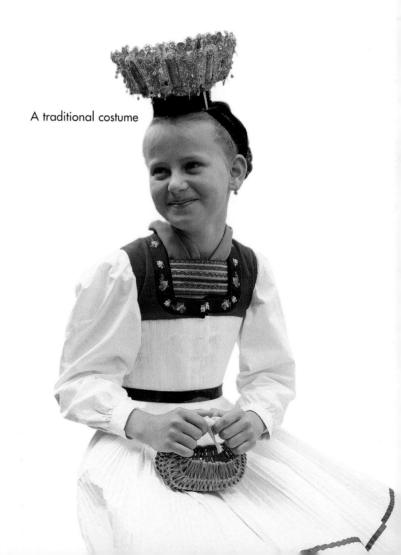

A Storybook Nation

A SACHERTORTE IS A CHOCOLATE LAYER CAKE SO RICH and creamy that one bite will make a chocolate-lover's heart

A Sachertorte

sing. The cake was invented about 150 years ago by a chef who worked for the Sacher Hotel in Vienna, Austria. For generations this world-famous pastry was served only in the Sacher Hotel's dining room. Then, in the 1960s, a rival Vienna café copied the ingredients and came up with its own version of the Sachertorte. When the Sacher Hotel sued in court—and won its case—

the legal battle made front-page news in Vienna newspapers. Why all this fuss over a cake? Because this is Austria, where good food is taken very, very seriously.

In the early 1800s, Johann Strauss Sr. was a popular band-leader in Vienna. Hoping his son, Johann Strauss Jr., would find a more stable profession than music, the father urged the boy to become a banker. Bowing to his father's wishes, Johann Jr. took a job as a bank clerk. But at night the younger Strauss

Opposite: **The village of Going**

A monument to Johann Strauss Jr. in Vienna's city park

Austrians gather for the Corpus Christi parade.

wrote waltzes and conducted his own small orchestra. Did the people of Austria condemn Johann Jr. for defying his father? No. Strauss waltzes have charmed the world for years. In Austria, music is taken very, very seriously too.

Enjoying the fine things in life has always been a serious business in Austria. The people have a passion for art, food, craftsmanship, sports, and especially for music.

Long ago, Austria was continental Europe's largest and richest empire. Over the ages, artists and architects from every corner of that empire traveled to its central cities to work their crafts. As a result, the towns of modern Austria are living museums, crammed with art treasures and alive with history.

The nation today is composed of dozens of ethnic groups, united primarily by the German language and the Roman Catholic faith. Austrians honor their past in folk festivals. During these festivals, men and women wear traditional peasant costumes and dance in the village squares to celebrate their glorious history. Austria is a storybook place of castles and kingdoms. It is also an uncommonly beautiful land where music is written on the winds.

Geopolitical map of Austria

A Land That Inspires

OUTSIDE VIENNA SPRAWLS A WILDERNESS OF BEECH AND fir trees called the Vienna Woods. In the early 1800s, a short, stocky man hiked there just about every morning. As he walked, he seemed to be in a trance—a dreamlike state. That man was Ludwig van Beethoven, and he composed music in a little notebook while tramping along paths in the Vienna Woods. One of his greatest symphonies, the Sixth or Pastoral Symphony, was written in this manner. Listen to Beethoven's Sixth and you will hear the changing moods of the forest—the morning sunlight bursting through the treetops, the fury of a sudden storm.

Opposite: **A village in the province of Salzburg**

The Vienna woods

The Vienna Woods is only one patch of beauty in the lovely land of Austria. Mountains and hills ripple in waves over its landscape, and farms nestle in its vast forests. Austria's beauty inspires art, music, and poetry, as Beethoven knew. Each year, millions of modern visitors come to enjoy all the wonders of Austria.

The Crossroads of Europe

A glance at a map shows that Austria lies pretty much in the middle of continental Europe. Because of its central location, merchants and migrants have trekked over the country for centuries. Two land features served as funnels to direct travelers through Austria. The Brenner Pass, a gap in the towering Alps Mountains, lies in the southwest. Since the days of ancient Rome, the Brenner Pass has been a major link

The Modern Brenner Pass

Today, a highway and a high-speed railroad run through the Brenner Pass, speeding travelers between Innsbruck, Austria, and Bolzano, Italy. The first railway through this gateway in the Alps was completed in 1867. The highway, called the Brenner Autobahn, features the modernistic Europa Bridge, which spans the Sill River Valley.

The State Opera House in Vienna

between Italy to the south and the Germanic lands to the north. The Danube, Europe's second-longest river after the Volga, flows through the northern part of Austria. It has been a highway for boats and traders for ages.

Austria shares borders with eight countries. To the west are Switzerland and the tiny nation of Liechtenstein. Germany is situated to the northwest, the Czech Republic is to the north, Slovakia and Hungary are on the east, and Italy and Slovenia lie to the south.

A small country, Austria spreads over 32,375 square miles (83,845 square kilometers). This makes Austria about the size of the U.S. state of South Carolina. Austria is shaped somewhat like a hand mirror, with a long narrow handle stretching westward. Its greatest distances are 355 miles (571 km) east to west, and 180 miles (290 km) north to south. Vienna is Austria's capital and its largest city.

Austria's Geographical Features

Area: 32,375 square miles (83,845 sq km)

Largest City: Vienna

Highest Elevation: Grossglockner, 12,457 feet (3,797 m) above sea level

Lowest Elevation: Neusiedler Lake, 377 feet (115 m) below sea level

Longest Navigable River: Danube

Largest Glacier: Pasterze Glacier

Largest Lake: Neusiedler Lake

Major Mountain Ranges: North Tyrol Alps, Salzburg Alps, Hohe Tauern, Ötztal Alps, Zillertaler Alps, Carnic Alps, Karawanken Mountains

Main Mountain Passes: Brenner and Plöcken (to Italy); Loibl (to Slovenia)

Austria is divided into nine provinces: Burgenland, Carinthia, Lower Austria, Salzburg, Styria, Tyrol (also spelled Tirol), Upper Austria, Vienna (the city), and Vorarlberg. These historic regions are separated by mountains in most cases. Over the years, the provinces have developed distinct personalities.

Diamond Lakes and Lofty Mountains

Mountains cover more than three-fourths of the Austrian landscape. The Alps, the great spine of Europe, rise in the western and southern half of the country. To the north is the Alpine Forelands, a sprawling valley studded by hills and low mountains. North of the Alpine Forelands is a separate mountainous area called the Granite Plateau. This plateau is made up of granite mountains and rich forests.

The Arlberg region of the Austrian Alps

A Mountain Wonderland

A popular song hails Innsbruck as a "beautiful Alpine town." Situated amid snowcapped mountain peaks, the town has long attracted Austrian royalty. Its most famous building is the *Goldenes Dachl* (Golden Roof)—a mansion built in the 1420s for Duke Friedl. Gossip at the time held that the duke, who was from a fabulously wealthy family, had gone broke. Behind his back, people called him Friedl the Penniless. To counter the rumors of his poverty, Friedl built a house with a golden roof. Actually, the roof consisted of copper tiles plated with gold. The house still stands and is a landmark in this mountain city.

Pasterze Glacier

Some Austrian mountains are actually glaciers—huge masses of ice that slide slowly over land. The Stubaital Valley in Tyrol Province has no fewer than eighty glistening glaciers. The biggest mountain of ice in the nation is the Pasterze Glacier. This glacier stands near the Grossglockner, Austria's highest mountain. People ski on the glacier slopes as late in the year as mid-June.

The Inn River

The Danube is Austria's major river. Almost all of the nation's streams and rivers empty into it. Within Austria's borders, the Danube is 217 miles (350 km) long and flows west to east along the northern half of the country. Other important rivers are the Drava, the Enns, the Inn, the Mur, the Mürz, the Traun, and the Salzach. These rivers are fed primarily by snow melting from the Alps.

Looking at Austria's Cities

Graz, the capital of the province of Styria and Austria's second-largest city, is located on the Mur River about 30 miles (50 km) from the border with Slovenia. It stands at an altitude of 1,115 feet (340 m). The average daily temperature in the city is 26.2° Fahrenheit (–3.2° Celsius) in January and 65°F (18°C) in July, and the average annual precipitation is 33.5 inches (85 centimeters). Graz is a university town with a student population that numbers 40,000. Over the years, six Nobel Prize–winners have taught or studied at Graz's world-famous university. Aside from its university, Graz has delightful parks and lovely architecture. Not to be missed is the city's Armory (above), a museum that houses hundreds of suits of armor and ancient swords. About 232,150 people live in Graz.

Linz is 100 miles (160 km) west of Vienna at an altitude of 1,000 feet (305 m). The city's average daily temperature is 28.6°F (–1.9°C) in January and 65.7°F (18.7°C) in July, and its average annual precipitation is 34.2 inches (87 cm). Linz's Hauptplatz, or main square, dates from the thirteenth century and holds the Trinity Column, built in 1723. The Alter Dom, a seventeenth-century cathedral, is another well-known landmark. Approximately 203,000 people live in Linz.

Set in a spectacular backdrop, Salzburg (below) spreads over both banks of the Salzach River and is nestled between two towering mountains. Its roots can be traced back some 2,000 years. In the sixteenth and seventeenth centuries, when its cathedral and many churches and fountains were built, Salzburg enjoyed great wealth. Then, in the eighteenth century, Salzburg slipped into a brief period of poverty, and the people worked to preserve their old buildings rather than build new ones. As a result, Salzburg today is an outstanding example of baroque architecture. Its most famous son is Wolfgang Amadeus Mozart. Stores in Salzburg sell sticky candies in wrappings that bear the great composer's likeness. In July and August, the world's greatest musicians come to perform in Salzburg's Mozart Festival. The average daily temperature in the city is 28°F (–2°C) in January and 65°F (18°C) in July, and the city gets 47.3 inches (120 cm) of precipitation in an average year. About 144,000 people live in Salzburg.

The Danube River in the state of Lower Austria

About 150 years ago, Johann Strauss Jr. wrote what was perhaps his most famous waltz, "On the Beautiful Blue Danube." Millions of people still dance to this lively and spirited tune. However, the title is only partially true. No one denies the river's compelling beauty, but the Danube is not blue. Depending on the light, its waters look either muddy brown or greenish. Still, a boat trip through Austria's Danube Valley, with castles and ancient river towns on both banks, is a must for all visitors.

Austria is a land of sparkling lakes tucked gently into the mountains. The southern province of Carinthia alone has more than 1,200 lakes. A famous lake district in Carinthia is called the *Funf Schwesterseen* (Five Sister Lakes). The largest of the Five Sisters is the Wörther See, which is about 10 miles (16 km) long. People swim in the Wörther See's warm waters from May to October. Boats of all descriptions bob in the large lakes of the Carinthia lake district.

The Danube, Europe's Highway

Aside from its striking beauty, the Danube is also Europe's superhighway for boat traffic. Beginning in the Black Forest in Germany, the Danube flows 1,777 miles (2,860 km) to the Black Sea. In all of Europe, only Russia's Volga River is longer. Some thirty-five major port cities, serving eight countries, lie along its banks.

Jewel of the Danube

Danube boats carrying tourists regularly stop at the ancient town of Melk in the province of Lower Austria. Rising dramatically from a bluff over the Danube is Melk's Benedictine Abbey, perhaps the most spectacular monastery in all of Austria. A church has occupied this site in Melk for almost 1,000 years. The inside walls and ceilings of the present Benedictine Abbey (completed in 1738) are alive with paintings of soaring angels and marching saints. Each year about half a million tourists come to walk the quaint streets of Melk and visit its remarkable church.

For hundreds of years, small villages on Austria's lakeshores survived on fishing and farming. Today, those lake towns are crowded with tourists. The tiny village of Maria Wörth sits on the tip of a wooded neck of land that juts into the Wörther See. The village has two churches that date back to the twelfth century. Maria Wörth is so picturesque that it is said to be the most photographed village in all of Austria.

The largest lake lying entirely within Austria's borders is Neusiedler Lake, in the east. Lake Constance, one of western Europe's biggest lakes, is on the western tip of Austria and spreads into Switzerland and Germany. A region called the Salzkammergut (the name refers to the ancient salt mines in

the area) in Upper Austria is another famous lake district. In the Salzkammergut, some seventy lakes are strung across the landscape like diamonds on a necklace.

Salzkammergut is known for its many scenic lakes.

"The Hills Are Alive . . ."

The Salzkammergut lake district was the setting for the Oscar-winning movie *The Sound of Music* (1965). Based on a Broadway play, the movie tells the story of a courageous woman who escapes with her family from the Nazis during World War II (1939–1945).

Many critics considered the play to be too sentimental, but the movie adaptation became one of the most popular films in cinema history. A bright musical score and the lovely Salzkammergut scenery no doubt added to the film's appeal.

The Rhythm of the Seasons

There is no mistaking the Austrian seasons—summer, winter, spring, and fall. Each season is distinct, but they vary from place to place thanks to the country's many mountain ranges. Southern Austria's climate is similar to that of Europe's hot and sunny Mediterranean region, while the north is colder and wetter, more like central Europe. Mountains create the divide that gives northern and southern Austria different weather patterns.

Skiing in the Austrian mountains is a very popular winter sport.

Generally, the climate is pleasant in Austria. January temperatures average 27°F (–3°C), while July temperatures average 67°F (19°C). In the north, occasional cold spells may last many days, and cloud cover and persistent drizzle can be annoying in the winter and fall. Farmers love the foehn, a warm, dry wind that comes up from the south and melts the winter's snow. City dwellers, however, claim the foehn puts people in a foul mood. Some Austrians say that headaches and even suicides increase when the foehn blows.

Austrians do not hibernate in the winters. Fresh snow turns their mountainous regions into winter wonderlands, to the delight of skiers and sledders. The winter sports season begins in December and lasts until April. It is no wonder that Austrian athletes excel in the Winter Olympics year after year.

Austria usually has ample rain to grow crops and flowers, though the rain falls unevenly over the country. The western regions of Austria get an average of 40 inches (102 cm) of rainfall each year. Eastern Austria has less rainfall because the Alps block moisture-carrying clouds. Still, there is plenty of rain to nourish Austria's exciting world of nature.

Avalanches

Skiers from all parts of the world flocked to the alpine towns of Galtür and Valzur in February 1999. Never had the winter landscape looked more beautiful in these Tyrol resort centers. But in one shocking twenty-four-hour period, two separate avalanches roared down from the mountaintops and dumped thousands of tons of snow on the villagers and the vacationers. The deadly snowslides arrived with no warning. Afterward, rescuers pulled thirty-eight bodies from the wreckage of the two towns.

Miraculously, a four-year-old boy was discovered alive by a rescue dog. The boy was near death when he was dug out of the snow, but he was playing with a ball within hours of his rescue.

Natural Treasures

Austria is a crowded country where human beings have farmed and built villages for thousands of years. You might think that overcrowding and many centuries of human settlement would simply squeeze plants and animals out of the Austrian landscape, but this is not the case. Austria enjoys a rich and varied natural world.

Forested Mountains

Huge wilderness areas are left undisturbed in Austria because the government has set them aside as national parks and nature areas. The law forbids building roads, houses, and factories in these preserves. Also, it is simply impossible to tame the tall mountains. Cities and farming villages developed long ago in the valleys, and, even in mountainous areas, practically every level spot has been farmed. But there are few level spots in Austria's highlands, and nature is free to work its magic in the mountain ranges.

Austria is the most densely forested nation in central Europe. Woodlands and meadows cover more than two-thirds of the country. Styria is called the "Green Province" because forests blanket most of its land. Trees and plant life tend to change with altitude. Willows and poplars grow along the Danube River and other lowland riverbanks. Beeches and firs stand in the valleys and on the low slopes, while spruce, pine,

The Rare and Shy Edelweiss

The edelweiss is a plant with small, brilliant yellow flowers that grow in clusters of two to ten flowerheads. The alpine edelweiss is especially beautiful, but it is a rare plant that grows in high, wild regions and seems to want to hide from human admirers. Every spring, Austrians comb the highlands hoping to catch a glimpse of the edelweiss flower in full bloom. Some people have hiked in the Austrian countryside for a lifetime without once seeing the treasured edelweiss.

Mushrooms

Wild mushrooms grow in thick clusters in the Vienna Woods. A favorite activity for city families is *Schwammerlsuchen*—mushroom hunting. With baskets in hand, families descend on the meadows of the woods early in the morning. Kids have lively and noisy contests to see who can gather the most wild mushrooms.

and larch grow on the upper slopes. Mountain peaks are virtually treeless, but grasses, berries, and, in the spring, a blaze of wildflowers grow above the timberline.

The Austrian government strives to keep the country green. Few nations have environmental laws as strong as those in Austria. Recycling is compulsory. Glass, cans, and paper garbage are kept separate and sent to recycling mills. Fast-food restaurants are encouraged not to serve food in wasteful containers.

The Vienna Woods stretch from the city of Vienna to the Alps. In the German language, the city of Vienna is *Wien*, and the Vienna Woods is the *Wienerwald*. It is the nation's largest forest, covering more than 700 square miles (1,812 sq km). The region was declared an Austrian National Park in 1905. The woodland is laced with hiking trails that lead to historic villages. Groves of beech, Norwegian pine, and oak rise in this great forest where many trees are centuries old. In the spring, the meadows are carpeted with a pleasant white flower called the ramson.

Another popular wilderness area is the Hohe Tauern National Park, which spreads over three provinces—Salzburg, Carinthia, and Tyrol. The park has 300 mountains, 246 glaciers, and Austria's highest mountain, the Grossglockner. The most spectacular feature of Hohe Tauern National Park is the Krimmler Falls, a three-step waterfall that is Europe's highest. Some 700,000 visitors a year come to the Hohe Tauern National Park.

Hohe Tauern National Park

Take a Hike

An estimated 35,000 miles (56,326 km) of hiking trails wind over Austria's lovely landscape. A particularly challenging footpath runs over mountain peaks from Bokstein, in Salzburg Province, to Mallnitz, in Carinthia Province. This ancient mountain trail takes walkers up steps made of flat stones that were put in place by Celtic people thousands of years ago. Austrian hikers do not shrink from venturing on treks that take two days or more. Many carry tents on backpacks and camp along the way. Others stay in travelers' dormitories that stand along countryside trails. The Austrian Alpine Club maintains 500 such dormitories in the Eastern Alps alone.

A male fallow deer

Wildlife in a Crowded Land

Normally, wildlife cannot thrive in a crowded country because human activity destroys the animals' habitat. But due to careful conservation measures and the unspoiled nature of the mountains, Austria's wild animals enjoy health and their numbers are increasing.

The Vienna Woods is home to the fallow deer, an especially beautiful and graceful deer that grows to be about 3 feet (90 cm) tall. The fallow deer originally lived along the Mediterranean Sea, but herds pushed their way up to

Austria. In remote mountain areas, European red deer are also found. These deer are often called the elk of Europe because they look somewhat like smaller versions of American elk. Wild boars, which look like domestic pigs, live in some wooded areas. Shy animals, wild boars are rarely seen in the wild.

Wild boars

An ibex is a mountain goat
with large curved horns.

Another rare creature found in the Austrian forests is the brown bear. The ibex, a mountain goat with curved horns, lives in alpine mountains, as does the chamois, which resembles an antelope. The chamois can leap over wide ravines in one graceful bound.

The Mythical Beast

In the main square of the southern Austrian town of Klagenfurt stands the statue of a ferocious-looking dragon called the *Lindwurm*. The statue was put up in the sixteenth century to honor a myth. According to the myth, such a dragon once lived there and terrorized the people until it was killed by a local hero. The statue is a favorite with small children, who pretend to be afraid of its grotesque face.

Small animals abound in Austria's forests and meadows. Squirrels and rabbits are common. Foxes live in the forests, but these swift animals are rarely seen. The pine marten makes its home in hollow trees, feeding on mice, rabbits, and birds. The marmot, the largest member of the squirrel family, is found in Hohe Tauern National Park. Signs in four languages forbid feeding the animals in the parkland.

Two marmots frolic in a field.

Birds of endless varieties soar over Austrian skies, and many Austrians are experts at identifying their calls. The golden oriole sings a pleasant song from the tops of poplars and fir trees. The river warbler makes a cranky sound, like an old sewing machine. The hammering of the great spotted woodpecker echoes through the Vienna Woods. Blackbirds of all kinds chatter in Vienna's many parks.

Flocks of waterfowl reside in Austria's lakes. No less than 300 species of waterbirds live on Neusiedler Lake (also called the *Neusiedler See*) in Burgenland Province. Neusiedler Lake is Austria's largest lake, but it is rarely more than 6 feet (1.8 m) deep, even in the center. The lake's many reed-filled marshes harbor an unusual bird life. The bittern, a rare heron, nests on the lake and calls out with a deep throaty song that sounds like a foghorn. Large families of graylag geese float on the waters. Other birds at Neusiedler Lake include the white spoonbill, the coot, the black-tailed godwit, the great reed warbler, and the gray heron.

The town of Rust on the shore of Neusiedler Lake has had a special relationship with birds for years. Just about every house on Rust's main street has a stork nest in its chimney. Every May, huge storks come from their winter nesting grounds in North Africa to this little town on the lake. They have flown more than 1,000 miles (1,609 km), yet each stork reclaims the same chimney nest it had the previous year. Homeowners in Rust recognize their own storks and regard them as old friends. The mother stork lays her eggs, and, in

September, the whole family takes off for North Africa again. They will return next year—to their old friends in Rust.

The region near Rust is famous for its palaces and old churches. It is a historic area, like just about all of Austria. The country has a rich past that dates back thousands of years.

A white spoonbill

The Saga
of an Empire

36

ALL FAME IS FLEETING, SAYS AN OLD PROVERB. AUSTRIA was once the most powerful empire in central Europe. At its zenith, the riches of the world flowed into the great empire. Over time, Austria lost its empire and became a comparatively small country. But the nation never lost its fame as a place of graceful living where citizens and visitors alike can enjoy high culture worthy of kings and queens.

Opposite: **An ancient Celtic sculpture**

Early Years

Human beings have lived in what is now Austria for many thousands of years, but historians know little about the earliest inhabitants. A tiny stone statue found in central Austria is believed to be 30,000 years old. Called the *Venus of Willendorf*, the statue depicts a woman with enormous breasts. The *Venus of Willendorf* was probably a fertility goddess—a figure that women prayed to so that they might have healthy babies. The statue is now displayed in the Natural History Museum in Vienna.

The Iceman

In 1990, in the snow-covered Alps that form Austria's border with Italy, a group of hikers came across the frozen body of a man. Constant subfreezing temperatures had preserved the body so well that even the pores of his skin were visible. The corpse was taken to Innsbruck University, where scientists determined that the man had lived at least 5,500 years ago. He carried many intriguing items, including a bow and arrow and a copper ax. Why he died alone and far from any known primitive settlement is a mystery.

Celtic relics found near Hallstatt

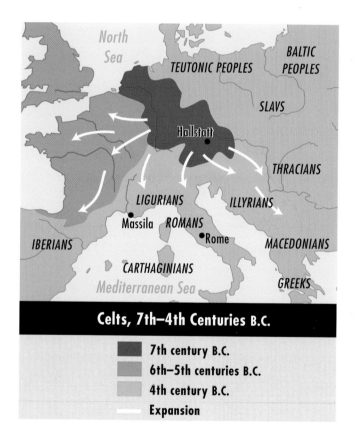

Celts, 7th–4th Centuries B.C.

- 7th century B.C.
- 6th–5th centuries B.C.
- 4th century B.C.
- Expansion

Shards of pottery and tools indicate that a prehistoric village—perhaps Austria's first town—existed where the small city of Hallstatt now stands. Celtic people lived at Hallstatt at least as early as 800 B.C. The Celts were among the first people in Europe to make iron. Ancient iron figures and wooden tools from that long-ago village can be seen today at Hallstatt's Prehistory Museum. In about 400 B.C., a Celtic tribe called the Vendi established an outpost on the Danube River. That tiny outpost later became Austria's capital city of Vienna.

Soldiers and merchants from mighty Rome came, and by 15 B.C. the Roman Empire controlled what is now Austria.

The ruins of a Roman temple in Austria

The Romans trekked through the Alps via the Brenner Pass and blazed a footpath over which the Brenner Autobahn runs today. For more than 400 years, Austria was a northern territory of the vast Roman Empire.

The Roman Empire collapsed in the A.D. 400s, and people from Germany to the north and from Slavic lands to the east entered Austria. In 955, Austria came under the rule of the Germanic King Otto I,

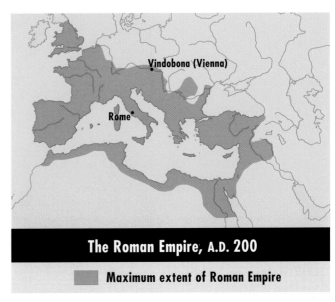

The Roman Empire, A.D. 200

    Maximum extent of Roman Empire

Roman Ruins in Vienna

The *Hoher Markt*, an ancient marketplace, is in the oldest section of Vienna. The neighborhood was heavily bombed in World War II. While clearing away the rubble from the bombing, workers discovered the foundations of several 2,000-year-old houses erected by the Romans. The ruins were preserved and may be seen there today. The Romans called the city Vindobona.

who later headed a loose confederation of states known as the Holy Roman Empire. Otto I was the first of a succession of German kings to reign over Austrian lands. Under the rule of German kings, the German language spread.

Enter the Habsburgs

For generations, a powerful family called the Habsburgs lived in Switzerland. In 1273, Rudolf I, a member of the Habsburg clan, was named Holy Roman emperor. Five years later, Rudolf defeated a rival in battle and took control of Vienna and the surrounding lands. For the next 650 years, the Habsburgs ruled Austria. No other European nation enjoyed such an unbroken dynasty.

The Habsburgs displayed a special kind of brilliance. They were able to expand the family's power more through marriage

Rudolf of Hapsburg Taking Possession of Austria

than through war. When necessary, the Habsburgs fought to maintain their empire, but they usually married off their sons and daughters to royal families throughout Europe. An old saying went, "Let others make wars, thou happy Austria. Marry!"

In 1496, the Habsburg emperor Maximilian I arranged for his son to marry the daughter of a Spanish king, thus extending Habsburg influence into Spain. The Habsburgs eventually divided into Spanish and Austrian branches. In 1521, the Habsburg king Ferdinand I married Princess Anne, sister of the king of Bohemia and Hungary. In this manner, the Austrian Empire, with a Habsburg at its head, spread to the east.

Keeping the empire together, however, led to war. A devastating conflict called the Thirty Years' War began in 1618, when many Austrians broke away from the Catholic Church and embraced the Protestant religion. The Habsburgs, who were Catholic, objected to the inroads of a new faith. A war erupted that lasted three decades and involved most of the nations of Europe. The Peace of Westphalia ended the Thirty Years' War in 1648 and allowed the Habsburg leaders to impose Catholicism on their subjects. Meanwhile, Turkish warlords, called the Ottomans, wanted the lands of Hungary and Austria. In 1529, and

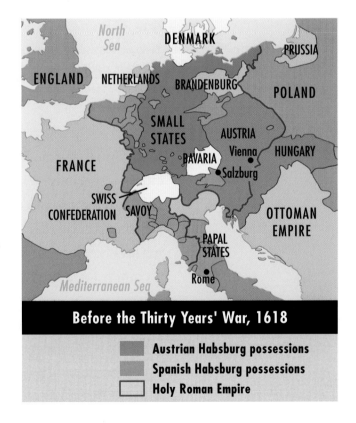

Before the Thirty Years' War, 1618

- Austrian Habsburg possessions
- Spanish Habsburg possessions
- Holy Roman Empire

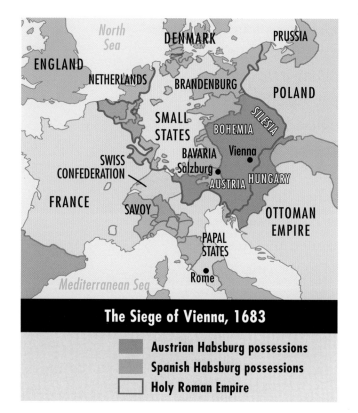

The Siege of Vienna, 1683

Austrian Habsburg possessions
Spanish Habsburg possessions
Holy Roman Empire

again in 1683, Turkish armies swept through Hungary and advanced up to the walls of Vienna. The 1683 siege of Vienna was broken with the help of Polish and German soldiers.

The Glories of Empire

Austria was far from being a nation in the modern sense. Instead, it was a confusing collection of small states and dukedoms—all of them technically part of the Holy Roman Empire. That empire, as the French critic Voltaire once said, was "neither Holy, nor Roman, nor an Empire."

The powerful Habsburg family helped to forge a nation out of these many small states. In the process of nation-building, Austrian cities—especially Vienna—blossomed. Wealthy families from the outlying provinces moved to Vienna to be near the ruling Habsburgs. The rich families tried to outdo one another in building lavish palaces or in demonstrating their generosity by erecting a church for city parishioners. Riches produced more riches as palaces and magnificent churches rose in the Austrian capital.

The growth of Vienna took place during an exciting period of artistic expression. A new style of art called *baroque* appeared in Italy in the late 1500s. Soon baroque art and architecture swept Europe. Baroque architects embellished

Belvedere, a Baroque Masterpiece

Prince Eugene of Savoy became Austria's greatest military hero of the Turkish War when troops under his command drove the Turks from the walls of Vienna in 1683. As a reward, Prince Eugene was allowed to build a palace in Vienna. Designed by the baroque architect Johann Lukas von Hildebrandt, the first building in this grand palace complex was completed in 1716. The grounds consisted of two mansions facing each other and separated by a formal garden. Prince Eugene admired lions, so stone figures of sphinxlike lions stand guard in the garden. He did not like the Turks, however, and some statues show Turkish prisoners in chains. The castle is called the *Belvedere* (Beautiful View).

their structures with graceful curves, high-flying arches, and flamboyant designs on the outside walls. The interiors of baroque buildings were lavishly decorated with flowers, curlicues, marble statues, and some gold-plated statues.

Baroque architecture was a magnificent rebellion against the more orderly styles of the past. Two of the greatest baroque architects—Johann Bernhard Fischer von Erlach and Johann Lukas von Hildebrandt—worked in Vienna. Under the direction of these and other masters, baroque buildings rose with an explosion of twirls, twists, and gingerbread flourishes. The marvelous palaces and churches transformed Vienna into the European fairyland we know today.

The Austrian upper class graced its mansions with sculptures. Outside walls were adorned with stone gods, goddesses, mythical beasts, and muscular giants. The Kinsky Palace (completed in 1716), and the Schönbrunn Palace (1706) are fine examples of Vienna baroque buildings bristling with statues. Many of these grand private homes stand unchanged today. They now serve as embassies for foreign countries, or house elegant offices. In some cases, the descendants of the old royal families occupy a small apartment within the building.

Church of Saint Charles

A terrible plague struck Austria in 1712. The Habsburg emperor, Charles VI, made a vow that he would build a grand church in Vienna if only God would end the plague. The plague subsided, and the emperor kept his promise. Charles VI commissioned the baroque architect Johann Bernhard Fischer von Erlach to build a church dedicated to Saint Charles. The church stands today as a baroque jewel, one of the most imposing structures in all of Vienna.

Artists also flocked to Vienna during the baroque period. Masters such as Johann Michael Rottmayr and Daniel Gran painted frescoes on the walls of churches and glorious scenes on the church ceilings. Franz Anton Maulbertsch was a leading canvas painter of the time. Baroque painting is restless and exciting and uses bold colors. The artists tried to capture feelings in their works. Vienna's Museum of Baroque Art, located in the Belvedere Palace, holds a fascinating display of these paintings.

Of all the arts, none shone more than music in old Vienna. Wealthy Viennese families hired court composers to give lessons to their children and to write music designed to enhance the families' prestige. Rich patrons competed to employ the most talented court composer. As a result, Vienna became the musical capital of the world.

The composer Franz Joseph Haydn (1732–1809) was born near Vienna, and as a young boy he sang for the emperor. Haydn perfected the classical symphony form. He wrote more than 100 symphonies and 80 string quartets. Haydn also served as a teacher and the anchor for Austria's musical community. In Vienna, Haydn met the young Wolfgang Amadeus Mozart, and said of him, "[Mozart is] the greatest composer known to me either in person or

A portrait of Franz Joseph Haydn

by name." Still later, Haydn instructed a promising young composer from Germany, Ludwig van Beethoven, and claimed, "[Beethoven] will one day be considered one of Europe's greatest composers and I shall be proud to be called his teacher."

The atmosphere of Vienna acted as a magnet, attracting musical geniuses from around Europe. In the 1860s, Johannes Brahms moved from Germany to the Austrian capital because he considered Vienna the "musician's holy city." Franz Schubert, Anton Bruckner, Gustav Mahler, and Vienna's favorite, Johann Strauss Jr., all enjoyed their most productive periods while working in Austria's capital city. For 200 years, Vienna reigned unchallenged as Europe's musical heart.

Guilty of Impersonation

Composers in Austria were once idolized as movie stars are in today's world. One night, the police outside Vienna caught a disheveled-looking man wandering about the woods. The man, who was ill-tempered, grumbled his name, "van Beethoven." Outraged, the police arrested him. The nerve of this tramp, claiming he was the great Beethoven! However, the police did not know that Beethoven, then considered Europe's greatest composer, cared little about his personal appearance. He often did not change his clothes and had the gravy from yesterday's dinner still spilled over his vest. Beethoven remained in jail for three days until friends arrived and convinced the police chief that his untidy prisoner was indeed the renowned composer.

The Politics of Empire

The power of the Habsburg family increased during the War of the Spanish Succession (1701–1714), when Austria gained lands in Italy. A threat to the Habsburgs came as Emperor Charles VI grew old. Charles VI had three daughters but no sons. A European tradition, called Salic Law, prohibited women from inheriting a kingdom when the ruling monarch died. Charles VI defied Salic Law in a decree called the Pragmatic Sanction that made his oldest daughter, Maria Theresa, heir to the Habsburg throne. When her European neighbors resisted Maria Theresa's rule, the

War of the Austrian Succession (1740–1748) broke out. The war ended with Maria Theresa still in command of Austria and still head of the proud Habsburg family.

Maria Theresa (1717–1780) ruled Austria for forty years, and her reign is thought of as a golden age for the country. Under her leadership, a standing army was formed, roads were built, and power over the empire was centralized in Vienna. In 1776, she abolished torture and the death penalty. A public-education system began during her realm. She is often called "the mother of Austria."

Franz I and Empress Maria Theresa of Austria and Their Children **by Martin Meytens**

The Palace Fit for a Queen

Maria Theresa had sixteen children, and naturally needed a large home. So she built onto Schönbrunn Palace, just outside Vienna. When alterations were completed, the great palace had more than 1,200 rooms—plenty of space for the empress's family. It became the most famous palace in all of Europe. Grand state dinners were given in its dining room, balls were held in the Great Gallery, and concerts were presented in its Mirror Room. Today the Schönbrunn is one of Austria's most popular attractions.

In Austria at that time, as in most of Europe, royal and aristocratic people lived in luxury while peasants faced hard work, insecurity, and, at times, starvation. During the late 1700s, a movement blossomed in France that rocked European society. Chanting the words "Liberty, Equality, Fraternity," French commoners stormed castles and seized royal families. Kings and aristocrats were arrested and condemned to death by tribunals made up of farmers.

Victim of the Revolution

Marie Antoinette (1755–1793) was the youngest and favorite daughter of Maria Theresa. Following the Habsburg tradition of marrying into power, Marie Antoinette was wed to King Louis XVI of France when she was a teenager. As queen, Marie Antoinette was oblivious to the sufferings of the French peasants. When told the peasants had no bread, she said, "Then let them eat cake." During the French Revolution, Marie Antoinette was brought to trial and beheaded on the guillotine.

In 1799, the military genius Napoléon Bonaparte took power in France and promptly began waging war on his neighbors. His armies defeated Austrian forces in 1805 and in 1809, and the empire lost much of its territory. Revolutions continued in Europe until 1814, when a group of nations—the Congress of Vienna— met in Vienna and ushered in a temporary peace. The Congress of Vienna was dominated by Austria's foreign minister, Prince Klemens von

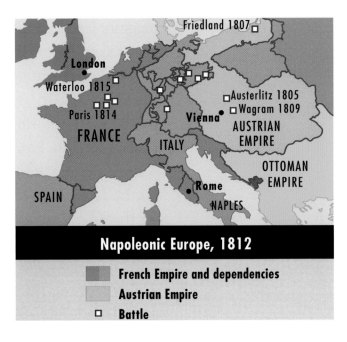

Napoleonic Europe, 1812

- French Empire and dependencies
- Austrian Empire
- □ Battle

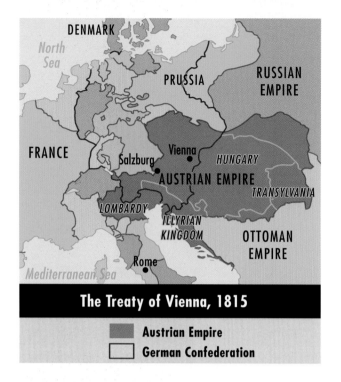

The Treaty of Vienna, 1815

- Austrian Empire
- German Confederation

Metternich (1773–1859), a bitter enemy of the revolutionaries. Hoping to put an end to the disorders, Metternich imposed police-state rule in Austria. However, rebellions broke out again in France in 1848, and the revolutionary fervor reached the Austrian Empire. Prince Metternich was forced to flee the country.

The political map of central Europe was redrawn in the wake of the revolutions. Both Italy and Germany transformed themselves from regions made up of patchwork principalities to modern unified nations In 1867, patriots in Hungary forced the Austrian emperor to accept what was called a Dual Monarchy, and Austria became Austria-Hungary. Under the Dual Monarchy, the people swore allegiance to one monarch who was both emperor of Austria and king of Hungary.

Leading Austria-Hungary was the Habsburg emperor Franz Josef (1830–1916). He was only eighteen when he took power in 1848. At the time, much of Europe was in great revolutionary turmoil. European leaders believed Franz Josef was too young and immature to rule a nation in such difficult times, but he proved his critics wrong. He provided wise leadership for the next sixty-eight years.

Austria in the Twentieth Century

Though Austria-Hungary was a huge territory that sprawled over central and southern Europe, it was never a unified country.

The empire included people of some twenty ethnic groups. The government recognized eight different languages, but a great many more languages were spoken in Austria-Hungary. The emperor's official title was "Emperor of Austria, King of Hungary, of Bohemia, Dalmatia, Croatia, Slavonia, Galicia, Lodomeria, and Illyria."

Ancient hatreds between ethnic peoples seethed in Austria-Hungary. Groups such as the Czechs and the Serbians wanted to split away from the empire and establish their own countries. This ethnic conflict within Austria-Hungary finally led Europe into war.

On June 28, 1914, Archduke Franz Ferdinand was touring the province of Sarajevo in an open car. Suddenly, a nineteen-year-old Serbian nationalist jumped on the running-board of the automobile. The nationalist pulled out a pistol and shot and killed both the archduke and his wife. Archduke Ferdinand was the nephew of Franz Josef and the man slated to become the next emperor of

Imperial Europe in 1871

Austro-Hungarian Empire

Archduke Franz Ferdinand and his wife in Sarajevo shortly before their assassination

Fatal Alliances

World War I was fought from 1914 to 1918. In terms of lives lost, it was history's second-bloodiest war, surpassed only by World War II. Two sides—the Allies and the Central Powers—fought in World War I. The Allies included France, Great Britain, Italy, Russia, the United States, and other countries. (The United States joined the war in 1917.) The Central Powers included Austria-Hungary, Bulgaria, Germany, and the Ottoman Empire (modern-day Turkey).

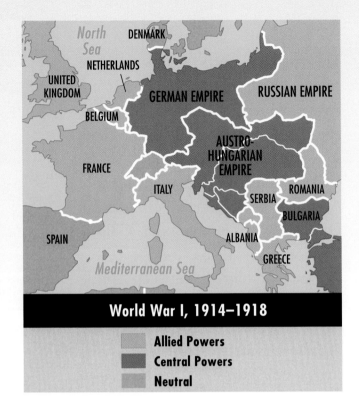

World War I, 1914–1918

Allied Powers
Central Powers
Neutral

Austria-Hungary. Furious over the assassination, Austria-Hungary declared war on Serbia. European nations at the time were entwined in a complex network of treaties, which required one nation to defend another in the event of war. Like falling dominoes, country after country mobilized troops, and World War I (1914–1918) began.

World War I ended with a disastrous defeat for Austria-Hungary and the Central Powers. The peace treaty at the end of the war dissolved the empire and created the new nation of Austria, which was about one-fourth the size of Austria-Hungary. The neighboring nations of Hungary, Czechoslovakia, and Yugoslavia were also formed. Austria emerged as a republic—

a nation with no king, queen, or emperor. Gone was the power of the Habsburg family, which had ruled Austria for almost 650 years.

Political chaos swept Austria in the years after World War I. Austrians looked for a leader who—like the emperors of old—would bring stability to their country. Many Austrians hoped Adolf Hitler (1889–1945), a one-time army corporal who headed a German political party known as the Nazis, would provide such leadership.

Hitler was born in 1889 in the Austrian town of Braunau, which lies across the Inn River from Germany. A troubled youth, he dropped out of school at age sixteen. The young Hitler fancied himself an artist, and traveled to Vienna to study. He was bitterly disappointed when he was not accepted at the leading art academy. Hitler stayed on in Vienna doing odd jobs, such as carrying suitcases at the train station. Vienna, then as now, was a city of many nationalities. All his life, Hitler had feared and distrusted foreigners, and while living in Vienna, he learned to hate Slavs and, especially, Jews.

After fighting in the German army in World War I, Hitler moved to Germany, where he became one of the early members of the Nazi Party. A fiery speaker, he rose to become chancellor (prime minister) of Germany in 1933. Hitler then built up the German army with the intention of expanding the nation. In 1938, he marched his army south and directed what was initially a bloodless conquest of Austria. Political unrest, which bordered on civil war, rocked Austria in the 1930s. Many Austrians hoped that Germany—and Hitler— would bring order to the country.

Adolf Hitler on his way to the town hall in Vienna

The German takeover of Austria was called *Anschluss* (union). It was heralded as the peaceful uniting of Germany with Austria. On the surface, the union seemed proper because Austrians were German-speaking and most considered themselves to be ethnic Germans. Non-Germans, however, such as the many Czechs and Poles living in Austria, were regarded as enemies.

Austrian Resistance to Germany

Many Austrians fought the German takeover of their country. One of those who resisted Anschluss was the Austrian chancellor, Engelbert Dollfuss. Dollfuss, who was also a dictator, was murdered by Austrian Nazis in 1934. The resistance movement continued throughout World War II as Austrian freedom fighters blew up German supply trains and fought German troops in the mountains. Approximately 3,000 members of the Austrian resistance were executed by the Germans. A small museum in Vienna called the Museum of the Resistance honors the Austrian patriots who fought Nazi rule.

Thousands of cheering Austrians lined the streets of Vienna in March 1938 to welcome Adolf Hitler as he paraded into the capital city to celebrate Anschluss. But that acceptance proved to be the most disastrous move the Austrian people made in the twentieth century.

Union with Germany put Austria in the grip of the Nazi dictatorship. An estimated 100,000 Austrians who disagreed with the Nazis were jailed as political prisoners. Austria's sizable Jewish population suffered terrible repression. Jews were forced to wear yellow Stars of David on their arms. They were not allowed to teach in universities or to practice law. Thousands of Jews fled the country. Many of those who remained were sent to concentration camps.

In 1939, Germany attacked Poland, plunging Europe into World War II. At first, the German army electrified the world as its tanks streaked into Poland and France and made deep penetrations inside Russia. Because of Anschluss, Austria was a vital part of this war machine. About 800,000 Austrian men were drafted into the army. After almost six years of war, 280,000 of them were dead and another 100,000

Austrians celebrating Anschluss in Salzburg in 1398

A Monument to Cruelty

Austria's largest concentration camp was a compound enclosed in barbed wire outside the town of Mauthausen on the Danube River. From 1938 to 1945, about 200,000 political prisoners and Jews were imprisoned in the camp, and more than half of them died there of brutal treatment and starvation. Some prisoners were thrown to their deaths from a high wall while guards called them "parachutists." Still others were executed in the prison's gas chambers. Today, tourists visit Mauthausen, where prisoners' living quarters and the gas chambers stand as grim reminders of that horrifying period.

Austrian soldiers returning home from Soviet prisoner of war camps after World War II

were listed as missing in action. Allied bombers pounded Austrian cities, killing more than 24,000 Austrian civilians. Much of Vienna was reduced to rubble, and some 270,000 Viennese were made homeless.

World War II ended in 1945 with the defeat of Germany and its allies. For the next ten years, Austria was an occupied country, divided into British, French, Soviet, and American zones. In 1955, the occupying forces withdrew, and Austria emerged as a neutral nation in the growing competition among Communist and non-Communist countries. Also in 1955, Austria joined the United Nations (UN).

Two major political parties—the People's Party and the Socialist Party (now the Social Democratic Party)—emerged in Austria. The country was often governed by a coalition of the two parties. Through the 1970s and the 1980s, the Socialist Party enjoyed a slight majority of votes.

Because it was a neutral nation, Austria served as a vital bridge between the Communist and non-Communist worlds. In 1969, the Soviet Union and the United States began a series of conferences—the Strategic Arms Limitation Talks (SALT)—in Vienna. SALT agreements were designed to limit weapons of mass destruction among the superpowers. The huge United Nations Center, a complex of office buildings, was built outside Vienna in the 1970s. Austria's neutrality made it an ideal spot for the UN facility.

Austrian diplomat Kurt Waldheim was secretary-general to the United Nations from 1972 to 1982. In this role, he participated in many important peacekeeping operations. He was also president of Austria from 1986 to 1992. Waldheim had been a German army officer in World War II. In the 1990s it was charged that, during the war, his army unit was involved with the killing of thousands of Yugoslavians and the deportation of Greek Jews. Waldheim and his backers denied any involvement in those atrocities.

The Austrian economy boomed in the 1980s and 1990s. Citizens enjoyed a superb school system and excellent health care. The days of empire are now consigned to the history books, and Austrians look forward to a bright future.

The Third Man

A famous British-made movie, *The Third Man*, was shot in Vienna in 1949. The movie involved post–World War II intrigue and spying. It also showed that Vienna was still a war-torn and rubble-strewn city four years after the end of the war.

Governing Austria

VISITORS TO AUSTRIA ARE IMPRESSED BY THE COUNTRY'S clean streets and roadways and its efficient public-transit systems. Clearly this is a nation that works. Austrians pay high taxes, but the country's governmental services—health care, education, and welfare—are the envy of other nations.

Opposite: **The Parliament Building in Vienna**

The Workings of the Government

Austria is a federal republic. Its nine provinces have self-governing responsibilities, but decisions that affect the entire country are made by the chancellor and the Parliament. The nation is a democracy, run by elected officials. All citizens above age nineteen are permitted to vote.

The Austrian National Anthem

The Austrian national anthem, which was adopted in 1947, sings praises to the country's astonishing beauty. The anthem is called *"Land der Berge, Land am Strome"* ("Land of Mountains, Land of Rivers"). The first verse of the anthem goes:

Land of mountains, land of streams,
Land of fields, land of spires,
Land of hammers, with a rich future,
You are the home of great sons.
A nation blessed by its sense of beauty.
Highly praised Austria.

Parliament Building

Both houses of the Federal Assembly meet in Vienna's impressive Parliament Building, which was erected in the late 1800s. In front of the building is a fountain featuring a huge statue of Athena, the Greek goddess of wisdom. It is hoped that Athena, wisest of all the gods, will counsel the members of Parliament to make wise decisions.

Residence of the President

The Hofburg Palace, a gracefully curving building in the heart of Vienna, was once the winter palace of the ruling Habsburg emperors. Today, the president of Austria lives there. Tourists flock to the Hofburg—not to see the president's apartment—but mainly because the palace serves as home for two of Vienna's main attractions—the Vienna Choir Boys and the Spanish Riding School.

President Thomas Klestil

The president of Austria is more of a figurehead than a national leader. The president appoints ambassadors, rides at the heads of parades, and greets foreign dignitaries. But he or she has little control over the country's Parliament and lacks the power to declare war. The president is elected by the people to a six-year term.

The chancellor, or prime minister, is the most important single person in Austria's government. In theory, the president appoints the chancellor, but in fact, the office goes to the head of the political party that gets the most votes. People do not vote for the individual candidate for chancellor, but for the party he or she represents.

The chancellor selects a cabinet whose members run various departments, such as the military and the education system. Cabinet members must be approved by the president. The most important day-to-day functions of the government are controlled by the chancellor and the cabinet.

Austria's Parliament is called the Federal Assembly. The Federal Assembly is made up of two houses: the *Bundesrat* (with 64 members) and the *Nationalrat* (with 183 members). The Bundesrat serves the nine provinces, while the Nationalrat is more national in scope. Nationalrat members are elected to four-year terms. Terms of the Bundesrat vary with the laws of their provinces. Usually the head of the majority political party in the Nationalrat is named chancellor.

The Nationalrat also has the power and the responsibility to vote "no confidence" in a government. This vote forces the chancellor and cabinet to resign and calls for new elections. The practice of calling for new elections is common among countries with a parliamentary system of government. Great Britain and many other European countries are governed by the parliamentary system.

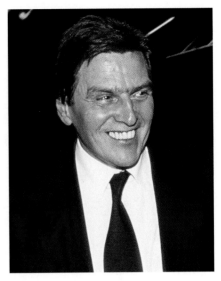

**Austrian chancellor
Victor Klima**

From Prisoner to Chancellor

Bruno Kreisky, who served as chancellor from 1970 to 1983, was born into a wealthy family that was close to the ruling Habsburgs. As a young man, however, Bruno became a socialist. He was also of Jewish heritage, which made him the target of Nazi oppression. Kreisky was imprisoned in the 1930s by the Nazi-led government. He rose from the prison experience to become one of Austria's most popular postwar chancellors.

Vienna (Inner Ring)

Vienna: Did You Know This?

Location: Northeast Austria, on the Danube River

Population: 1,539,848 (1991 est.)

Altitude: 653 feet (199 m)

Average Daily Temperatures: January, 29.5°F (−1.4°C); July, 63.9°F (17.7°C)

Average Annual Rainfall: 27 inches (69 cm)

Originally settled by Celts about 400 B.C., Vienna has been Austria's capital since 1918. Today, the city is also an important commercial, industrial, and cultural center.

Austria has an independent court system. Judges are expected to make decisions free of influence from political parties. The Supreme Court is the highest court in the land. Separate courts deal with juvenile crime and labor disputes. Austria has a special court whose job is to interpret the Constitution and make sure that no act of Parliament violates the Constitution's terms. Human rights that protect individual liberties are written into the Constitution.

NATIONAL GOVERNMENT OF AUSTRIA

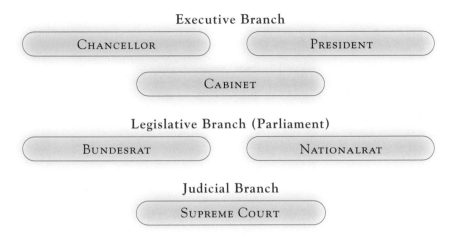

Executive Branch

CHANCELLOR   PRESIDENT

CABINET

Legislative Branch (Parliament)

BUNDESRAT   NATIONALRAT

Judicial Branch

SUPREME COURT

The Austrian Flag

The design of the Austrian flag is so old that it is linked to legend. According to legend, when Austrian duke Leopold V led his troops into battle in the year 1191, he fought so ferociously that his white coat was soaked with blood except for the part under his belt, which remained white. Therefore, to this day, the Austrian flag consists of three horizontal stripes of red, white, and red.

Each of Austria's nine provinces has legislative assemblies, called *Landtags*, and governors. Landtag members are elected by the people, and the Landtag chooses the governor. Tradition requires that each province retain some form of home rule, but provincial government must be conducted within the framework of Austria's Constitution.

Political Austria

Austria has two major political parties—the People's Party and the Social Democratic Party. Both parties support large-scale government programs to promote education and welfare, but they differ slightly in the methods used to pay for these programs. In the 1970s, the liberal Social Democratic Party—then known as the Socialist Party—was more popular. The more conservative People's Party has gained strength in recent years.

The Austrian Coat of Arms

A coat of arms is a symbol that used to be carved onto the shields or armor of a nation's warriors. Prominent on Austria's coat of arms is the figure of an eagle. Since the 1100s, Austria has been represented by an eagle with outstretched wings. In the years of the Dual Monarchy, Austria-Hungary had a double eagle as its coat of arms. The double eagle had two heads, one pointed west toward Austria, the other east toward Hungary. The present coat of arms was adopted by Parliament in 1945.

Political debate is often fiery in coffeehouses and on the street. Austrians will argue politics without end. Debate in Parliament can become particularly stormy. But if neither of the major parties has a clear majority, the Austrian people and their politicians are quick to accept compromise. Through most of the 1980s and 1990s, a coalition government—a cooperative arrangement between the People's Party and the Social Democratic Party—ruled Austria.

Two other parties consistently win seats in parliamentary elections. The Green Party represents Austria's strong conservation movement. Members of the Green Party object to nuclear power, defense spending, and anything that is likely to contaminate the environment. The Freedom Party takes a major stand against immigration. Many Austrians are disturbed about

the large numbers of immigrants, mostly from Eastern Europe, who are pouring into their country today. In 1994, the anti-foreigner Freedom Party won almost 23 percent of the votes.

In February 2000, Austria formed a new coalition government that gave the Freedom Party great power. Four months earlier, the party had won 27 percent of the vote in a parliamentary election. The formation of the coalition government caused an uproar in the European political community and elsewhere around the world. The problem? The Freedom Party was headed by Jörg Haider, a politician who was governor of Carinthia Province. In the past, Haider has made speeches praising Adolf Hitler, although he has since apologized for his statements. Many Europeans believe that Austrians were partners with the Nazis during World War II, rather than their victims. Because of the uproar, Haider resigned as head of the Freedom Party. However, no one can deny that Haider and the Freedom Party were legally elected and that the country remains a solid democracy.

Colorful Politics

If the party system gets confusing, a citizen can always vote by color. Each political party claims a color as its banner. The Social Democratic Party is red, the People's Party is black, the Freedom Party is blue, and the Green Party is, of course, green.

Education and Security for All

The Austrian government showers benefits on its citizens. Workers who are injured or who become ill collect disability pay. Pregnant women are given generous maternity leaves from their jobs. Elderly people receive pensions. A national health-insurance system provides free medical care. Because of these programs, few Austrians suffer hunger or homelessness.

A soldier in Salzburg

Austria maintains a citizen's army for national defense and to aid citizens in the event of national disasters such as floods or earthquakes. All able-bodied men must serve seven months of basic training. After basic training, the men become members of reserve units that can be called up in an emergency. A young man can avoid military service by opting to take a community-oriented job such as teaching. Traditionally, the Austrian military is male-dominated. Until 1998, women could not serve in the army, even on a voluntary basis. A law passed in 1998 now allows women to join the military.

Austria's commitment to public education is historic. As far back as 1867, laws required children to spend eight years in school. The emphasis on schooling has produced one of the best-educated societies in the world. Illiteracy is almost unknown in Austria.

Education from primary school through the university level is free. Laws require all children from ages six through fifteen to attend school. After elementary school, a student moves on to either a vocational high school to learn a trade, or a preparatory school for pre-college study. Austria has twelve universities and six colleges of fine art, serving more than 200,000 students. Three of the oldest and most famous universities in the country are Vienna (founded in 1365), Graz (1585), and Innsbruck (1677).

Historic High School

A secondary school in Vienna called the Schottegymnasium was founded by Catholic priests of the Benedictine order in the year 1155. The school still educates students today, making it one of the oldest (some say *the* oldest) continually operating high schools in the world.

The University of Vienna

The Economy at Work

D URING WORLD WAR II, AUSTRIA'S ECONOMY WAS devastated. Many of its factories were destroyed by bombs, and hundreds of farms were abandoned. Through hard work, the Austrian economy recovered in the 1950s. Austria is now one of Europe's most productive and prosperous nations.

Opposite: **Vineyards in a suburb of Vienna**

Cooperation and Productivity

Austria has few natural resources. Only small deposits of petroleum and natural gas have been found in the country. Even its coal, mined mainly in the province of Styria, is of poor quality. Because of its many mountains, only 17 percent of Austria's land surface is suitable for farming. The nation's most valuable resources are its forests, which produce wood and paper products, and its swift-running streams, which can be used to generate electricity.

Despite being resource-poor, Austria has a productive economy. Its unemployment figures are among the lowest of any industrialized country. The nation has achieved success largely through the quality of its workers. Austrians are superb craftspeople. Austrian industries concentrate on making quality products rather than on churning out mass-produced goods. Glassware, jewelry, and specialty clothing items made in Austria are among the world's finest.

Glassware being made by hand in Austria

Salt

Throughout its history, Austria has been rich in one resource—salt. Millions of years ago an inland sea covered Austria, and that ancient sea left vast salt deposits. The salt is found underground. Some salt deposits have been mined continuously for 4,000 years. Today, salt is used by the chemical industry. Modern tourists visit salt mines where miners once descended from level to level on polished wooden slides that are very much like the slides on a playground. Adventurous tourists can take a giddy ride on those old slides.

The government aids the economy with low corporate taxes and by promoting labor peace. Rarely does Austria suffer a major strike by workers that paralyzes an industry. Also, the government owns many key industries, including the railroads, and strives to keep charges low. The government advertises that the costs of operating a business in Austria are the lowest in all of continental Europe.

Manufacturing

In 1997, manufacturing employed more than 20 percent of the nation's total workforce. Vienna is the most

Resources

Industrial	C	Coal
Cereals	I	Iron
Cereals, Dairy	G	Graphite
General farming	L	Lead
Forests	O	Oil/Gas
Nonagricultural	S	Salt
	T	Tungsten

highly industrialized city. Many huge steel plants are located at Linz, and one of Europe's largest aluminum plants operates at Braunau. Leading manufactured products include automobiles, auto parts, locomotives, and machine tools. The chemical industry produces fertilizers and plastics and employs 23,000 workers.

These artists are designing a female marionette in Salzburg.

Hundreds of Austria's factories are small and specialize in handmade products that take great skill to create. The Augarten china factory in Vienna, for instance, has been making marvelous porcelain cups and plates since the year 1717. Some shops concentrate on making high-quality dolls. Pianos of concert-hall quality are carefully created in Vienna. Another Viennese plant specializes in making top hats. None of these handmade products is inexpensive. For example, the average top hat made in Vienna sells for U.S.$400.

What Austria Grows, Makes, and Mines

Agriculture (1995)

Sugar beets	2,886,000 metric tons
Corn (maize)	1,474,000 metric tons
Barley	1,065,000 metric tons

Mining (1995)

Iron ore	2,107,000 metric tons
Magnesite	783,000 metric tons
High-grade graphite	12,000 metric tons

Manufacturing (1995; *value added in Austrian schillings*)

Electrical machinery and apparatus	47.1 million
Nonelectrical machinery and apparatus	37.3 million
Beverages and tobacco products	31.0 million

Farming and Mining

Large-scale farming is difficult in Austria because the country is so mountainous. Most farms are small and family-owned. Although only 1.4 percent of the labor force works in agriculture, Austria grows more than 90 percent of its own food. The relatively flat Danube Valley is the nation's most productive farming region. Dairy cows and livestock graze in mountainous areas. Orchards, found mainly in the east, grow apples, pears, plums, and peaches. Grapes for the wine industry are grown near Vienna. Leading crops include sugar beets, corn, barley, potatoes, rye, and wheat. Local farms meet all of Austria's needs for meat and dairy products.

Mining employs fewer than 1 percent of the country's workers. Austria is a large producer of a substance called magnesite, which is made into bricks for the construction industry. Iron ore is mined at Eisenerz in the province of Styria. A huge mountain in Styria called Erzberg (Ore Mountain) is the source of much of the nation's iron ore. Other mines produce graphite, lead, zinc, and copper. But the lack of mineral resources is a drain on the Austrian economy. Austria must buy about 80 percent of its oil and half its natural gas from other countries.

Lipizzaner horses grazing on an Austrian stud farm

Transportation and Communications

Austria has about 3,500 miles (5,633 km) of railroad tracks, of which some 90 percent are owned by the state. More than half of the trains are electric. About 80,197 miles (129,061 km) of paved roads, including more than 1,000 miles (1,609 km) of major highways, crisscross the land. Twenty airports with paved runways are licensed in the country. The nation's largest airport is the Schwechat Airport at Vienna. The Danube River remains a major waterway for barge traffic carrying bulk cargo such as coal and iron ore. Major Danube ports are at Linz, Enns, Krems, and Vienna.

In order to lessen traffic jams and reduce pollution, Austria is committed to mass transit. Streetcars, buses, and trains are environmentally more friendly than automobiles. The government subsidizes trains and subways to keep ticket prices affordable.

A tram in the city of Graz

Getting Around in Vienna

Mass-transit riders in Vienna buy a weekly or a monthly pass that allows them to use the city's buses, streetcars, and subways. Ride the mass-transit system, and you might assume the service is free. There are no ticket-takers or turnstiles. People simply climb on board and take a seat, then get off when they reach their stop. However, inspectors sometimes board buses or streetcars and ask to see passengers' up-to-date passes. These inspectors' visits are rare, though, and ridership is really on the honor system. Few people cheat.

Austrians are such avid readers that thirty daily newspapers are sold at newsstands. Twenty-seven radios stations and forty-seven television stations are active in Austria today. And just about every family owns a television set and has a telephone.

A newsstand in Vienna

Money Facts

Austria's basic monetary unit is the schilling. A schilling consists of 100 groschen. There are coins of 5, 10, and 50 groschen and 1, 5, 10, and 20 schillings. Paper notes come in denominations of 20, 50, 100, 500, 1,000, and 5,000 schillings.

Austria honors its artists and scientists on its paper currency. Here are some examples:

- 20-schilling note—Moritz M. Daffinger (1790–1849), artist
- 50-schilling note—Sigmund Freud (1856–1939), founder of psychoanalysis
- 100-schilling note—Eugen Böhm-Bawerk (1851–1914), professor at the Academy of Sciences who served briefly as president
- 500-schilling note—Otto Wagner (1841–1918), architect

In January 1999, the European Union introduced a common currency—the euro— that is now being used by financial institutions in some member countries. There is a fixed exchange rate of 13.7603 Austrian schillings per euro. The euro will replace the local currency in consenting countries for all transactions in 2002. Austria's schillings will no longer be used after that time.

Trade, Finance, and the Service Industry

In ancient times, Austria was a crossroads nation dependent on foreign trade. Trading goods with neighboring countries remains an active enterprise. Since 1995, Austria has been a member of the European Union (EU), a group of fifteen Western European nations that cooperate to ease trade restrictions. The EU may soon lead, economically at least, to a "United States of Europe." Today, about two-thirds of all Austria's foreign trade is conducted with EU members. Germany, also an EU member, is Austria's largest trading partner. In all, Austria carries out trade with 150 nations. Austria exports its manufactured goods as well as its exquisite handcrafted items. Raw materials and some food products are imported.

More than 200,000 Austrians are employed in the finance and insurance sectors. The nation's banks grant loans for the construction of houses, hotels, and factories. Visitors from foreign countries go to banks to exchange their money for Austrian currency.

The cost of living in Austria is high—some people say, frightfully so. One way to compare costs with the United States is to eat lunch at one of the many McDonald's restaurants that have sprung up in Austria in recent years. If a Big Mac and fries cost $3 in the United States, you can bet that same lunch will run the equivalent of $5 to $6 in an Austrian McDonald's.

Tourists enjoy Austria's dramatic scenery.

The job of a service worker is to perform a service rather than produce goods. A restaurant cook, a hotel worker, and a bagger in a supermarket all hold service jobs. Sixty-seven percent of the Austrian workforce is employed in the service industries. Tourism, of course, is a large factor in the service business. Every year, foreign tourists add more than U.S.$1 billion to the Austrian economy.

A Look at
the Austrians

"To be Austrian is not a geographical concept but a spiritual idea, the idea of an ethically enlightened humanity springing from a combination of peoples and classes."

—*writer Oskar Bender, observing the Austrian people in 1936*

Opposite: **Vienna's flea markets are very popular.**

Who Are the Austrians?

Don't expect to see an "Austrian look" on the faces of people when you walk the streets of an Austrian city. Some Austrians are tall and blond, like many Germans and northern Europeans. Others are short and dark-skinned, like many Italians.

Austrians have a variety of ethnic backgrounds.

For thousands of years, various ethnic groups have settled in Austria and left their looks, as well as their marks, on the country. Many Austrians are a mixture of Germanic people from the north, Slavic people from the east, and Mediterranean people from the south.

Austrian Jews

Jews have lived in Austria for more than 1,000 years, but they have had a turbulent history there. In the 1400s, Jews were declared enemies of Christianity and were burned at the stake. In the 1600s, they were officially banned from the country. After the European revolutions of 1848, the restrictions on Jews were abolished. Jews gathered primarily in Vienna, where they formed a lively community of doctors, merchants, scientists, artists, and musicians. By 1910, Vienna held about 180,000 Jews, roughly 10 percent of the city's population. Then, in 1938, Adolf Hitler and the Nazis took over Austria. Jews were arrested and sent off to concentration camps where thousands of them died. Those Jews who could leave Austria fled, and Vienna's Jewish population shrank to a few hundred people.

About 12,000 Jews live in Vienna today. Vienna's Jewish Museum tells the story of the achievements as well as the persecution of Austria's Jews.

Though they are an ethnic mix, about 98 percent of the Austrian people speak German. Austrians use various dialects, or versions, of the German language. For example, people from the province of Vorarlberg, which borders Switzerland, speak a Swiss-German dialect called Schwyzerdütsch. Some

Multilingual shop signs in Salzburg

Common Phrases

Here are some common German words and phrases used in every province of Austria.

Bitte	Please
Danke.	Thank you.
Bitte sehr.	You're welcome.
Guten Abend.	Good evening.
Hier, da	Here, there
Wieviel?	How much?
Auf Wiedersehen.	Good-bye.
Sprechen Sie Englisch?	Do you speak English?
Wieviel kostet es?	How much does it cost?
Wo ist die Bahnhof?	Where is the train station?

Austrians claim they have difficulty understanding their fellow citizens from other provinces. This can be compared to a person from New York City failing to understand the English spoken by a person from rural Georgia. However, all Austrians can switch to High German, a unifying dialect, whenever they wish. English is studied in schools and serves as a second language when Austrians converse with foreign visitors.

The Foreign Community

About 600,000 foreign residents live legally in Austria. Unlike tourists, foreign residents are allowed to hold jobs. No one knows how many foreigners are working illegally in Austria. Most of the foreigners are from the east, mainly the former Yugoslavia and the former Soviet Union. Others come from Turkey and the Czech Republic. In the 1990s, civil war

Who Lives in Austria?

Austrian	93.4%
Citizens of former Yugoslavia	2.5%
Turkish	1.5%
German	0.7%
Other	1.9%

People from many different countries emigrate to Austria.

rocked Yugoslavia and the economy collapsed in formerly communist Russia. Seeking security and jobs, masses of Eastern Europeans moved to stable Western European countries such as Germany, Italy, and Austria.

Historically, Austria has been a place where different ethnic groups met and lived together in relative peace. However, the recent wave of immigrants has disturbed many Austrians. People complain that the newcomers don't speak German, that many are non-Catholic, and that their willingness to accept low-paying jobs drives down wages. This resentment of foreign workers is beginning to affect government policies. In the 1994 parliamentary elections, the once-small Freedom Party—which calls for limits on the numbers of foreign workers allowed in the nation—won a surprising 23 percent of the vote. The government responded by severely reducing entry permits to "guest workers." Continuing this trend, the Freedom Party won 27 percent of the vote in the 1999 elections.

Yet some Austrians welcome the influx of foreign workers because they do the jobs that native Austrians don't want to do. The foreigners wash dishes in restaurants, work in laundries, and scrub floors in hospitals. In addition to their labor, the immigrants have brought new foods and music to the country. In a Vienna flea market at the *Mexikoplatz* (Mexico Plaza), Eastern Europeans gather to exchange goods and talk about their homelands. Hand signals and body language prevail as Turks buy clothes from Russians, and Poles sell radios and televisions to Croatians. The smell of fried sausages from

Graz is Austria's second-largest city.

food vendors lingers in the air. The place is a babble of languages. Many Austrians, even those who might resent the foreign "invasion," come to the flea market on Sundays to enjoy its color and its food.

Where the People Live

The 1991 census counted 7,795,786 people living in Austria. In 1999, the estimated population stood at more than 8 million.

Population of Major Cities (1991 est.)

Vienna	1,539,848
Graz	232,150
Linz	203,000
Salzburg	144,000
Innsbruck	115,000

Austria is roughly the size of South Carolina, but it holds more than twice as many people as that American state. Because three-fourths of the country consists of mountainous areas where few people live, Austria is a crowded land with most of its people concentrated in pockets of cities and towns.

Roughly six out of every ten Austrians are city-dwellers. With more than 1.5 million residents, Vienna is by far the largest city. About 20 percent of Austria's total population lives in Vienna and its suburbs.

Austria has a stable population with little growth from year to year. Its population in 1991 was only about 300,000 more than the 1971 figure. Some 15 percent of the present population is over age sixty-five, indicating that Austrians enjoy excellent health and medical care. Life expectancy for an Austrian man is a little more than seventy-four years, and an Austrian woman can expect to live for more than eighty years. These figures make Austria one of the foremost nations in the world when it comes to living a long life.

Population distribution in Austria

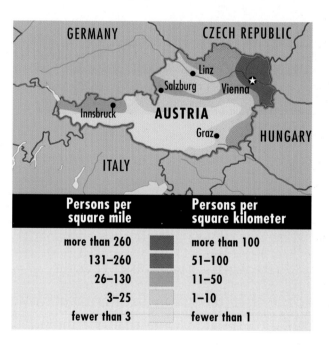

Persons per square mile		Persons per square kilometer
more than 260		more than 100
131–260		51–100
26–130		11–50
3–25		1–10
fewer than 3		fewer than 1

Ancient Illnesses

Austrians today enjoy good health, but this was not always the case. A terrible plague ravaged Austria and most of Europe in the 1600s. In the Vienna region alone, almost 100,000 people died of the sickness.

When the plague finally dwindled, Holy Roman emperor Leopold I (1640–1705) raised a monument in Vienna in gratitude to God. The *Pestsäule* (Plague Column) is now a Vienna landmark.

A People of Spirit

THE CITY OF SALZBURG IS WORLD FAMOUS AS THE BIRTH-place of the composer Wolfgang Amadeus Mozart. But on a certain morning in early December, few people talk about Mozart. Instead, everyone watches the grand Saint Nicholas Day Parade. Young men dressed in animal skins and wearing horned masks march down Salzburg's main street. Parents warn small children that the costumed figures, called *Krampus*, will eat them up if they don't behave. The warnings are all in fun because the real purpose of the scary-looking Krampus is to drive away evil spirits. The procession is sponsored by the Catholic Church, but its spirit is rooted in ancient mythology.

Opposite: **The Benedictine Abbey in Melk**

A man dressed as a Krampus for the Saint Nicholas Day Parade

Followers of Religions in Austria	
Roman Catholic	78%
Protestant	5%
Other	4.5%
None	9%
No response	3.5%

Saint Stephen's Cathedral

A Catholic Land

About 78 percent of the Austrian people are Roman Catholics, but there is no law that makes Catholicism a state religion. Protestants, Jews, and Muslims also live and worship in Austria. The Constitution guarantees freedom of religion to all citizens. Although the vast majority of Austrians cling to their old faith, church attendance has declined. A recent poll determined that only 12 percent of Austrian Catholics are regular churchgoers.

The center of Austrian Catholicism is at Saint Stephen's Cathedral in Vienna. The cathedral, which stands in the heart of old Vienna, rises as high as a modern office building. Streets radiate out from Saint Stephen's like spokes on a wheel. The foundation of the present church (it replaced an even older one) was laid in 1359. The building process went on for hundreds of years as various bishops added to the structure. Saint Stephen's is the most beloved building in Austria, and it is a privilege to be married or baptized there. Austrians call Saint Stephen's "Old Steffl."

A certain rhythm of life develops in nations where one religion dominates. This rhythm is evident in the holidays and periods of worship that take place every spring in Austria. *Fasching* (the pre-Lenten time of celebration) is followed by Lent (a period of sacrifice), and Lent is concluded by Easter (a day of joy to hail the resurrection of Christ). These events take place while church bells ring and carolers sing hymns. The Austrian calendar is studded with religious holidays.

The Scars of War

Saint Stephen's Cathedral is a symbol of peace and love, but the 500-year-old building bears the scars of war. More than 300 years ago, Turkish army cannons bombarded Saint Stephen's. It is believed that a Turkish cannonball, fired in the year 1683, is still lodged in an upper wall. In 1945 during World War II, bombs caused a fire that gutted the inside of the church and destroyed its roof and most of its outside walls. It took seven years to rebuild the cathedral.

Men participating in *Fasching* dress as women for the procession.

National Religious Holidays

New Year's Day	January 1
Epiphany	January 6
Easter Monday	Monday following Easter
Ascension Day	Thursday 40 days after Easter
Whitmonday	The seventh Monday after Easter Monday
Corpus Christi	Thursday after Whitmonday
Assumption of the Virgin	August 15
All Saints' Day	November 1
Immaculate Conception	December 8
Christmas Eve	December 24
Christmas Day	December 25
Boxing Day	December 26

A passion play is a spirited—some say agonizing—drama staged in many Catholic regions. The plays illustrate the sufferings and death of Christ and remind the audience that he died for the sins of humankind. The town of Thiersee in the province of Tyrol puts on a passion play every six years, and thousands of people come to see the drama. Thiersee has held passion plays since the 1700s.

The Scientist Monk

Gregor Johann Mendel (1822–1884) was born in Heinzendorf, Austria (now part of the Czech Republic), to a peasant family. As a boy, he wondered why some plants in his garden were short, others tall, and still others bloomed in dazzling colors. He often prayed to God, hoping to find answers to his many questions about plant life.

At the age of twenty, Mendel entered a monastery. Though he devoted his life to the church, he continued to study plants. Mendel concluded that plants inherit characteristics such as color and height from their parents in much the same manner as humans do. In 1866, he published what he had learned in a book, but his findings were ignored until 1900, when several other prominent scientists confirmed Mendel's conclusions. Today, Mendel is hailed as one of the founders of the science of genetics—the passing on of characteristics from parents to their offspring.

Christmas pastries in a
Vienna baker's shop window

Christmas in Austria

In Catholic tradition, the period of Advent begins four Sundays before Christmas. Advent, which means "a coming," is a time that reminds Christians that Jesus Christ will return to earth some day. In Vienna, Salzburg, Innsbruck, and other Austrian cities, Advent starts the Christmas season. Street markets, called Christmas Markets, open in select neighborhoods. Vendors sell home-cured hams and a hard gingerbread called *Lebkuchen*. Many of the vendors wear *Trachten*, or folk costumes, whose style dates back hundreds of years. Neighborhood churches hold concerts during Advent, and music and singing are heard everywhere.

December 6 is *Nikolo Day*, the special day when *Nikolo* (Saint Nicholas, or Santa Claus) visits children. Before they go to bed, small children leave their shoes in a selected spot in the house where Nikolo will be sure to find them. In the morning, the shoes are magically filled with gifts and candy. Parents warn children that if they are naughty, Nikolo will leave them only a lump of coal, but such a punishment is almost never imposed.

Strings of lights and rope covered with pine branches grace the streets as Christmas day approaches. Many ornaments on the pine branches are hand-painted globes showing smiling faces or playful animals. Austrians do not like mass-produced ornaments. Families prefer to make their own Christmas decorations. An Advent wreath is displayed in most households. The wreath is made of wire and covered by pine branches. The bottom of the Advent wreath holds four candles that are lit one by one on the four Sundays before Christmas.

Christmas trees go up in town squares. Some towns erect smaller trees decorated with breadcrumbs for the birds. Tourists are always present in Austrian cities, but it seems the

Silent Night

Certainly the most famous Christmas song throughout the world is "Silent Night, Holy Night." The song was written on Christmas Eve 1818 in the Austrian village of Oberndorf, about 13 miles (21 km) north of Salzburg. A legend says that a mouse ate through a belt on the church organ, rendering the organ useless.

We don't know if the mouse story is true. But we do know that a schoolteacher, Franz Gruber, worked with a local priest, Josef Mohr, to come up with a new song for Christmas-day services. That song was "Silent Night, Holy Night," which Christians around the world have been singing for almost 200 years.

foreign presence increases during the Christmas season. More French, Italian, and English is heard on the streets. Austrians celebrate Christmas in a very hearty manner, and foreigners come to catch the spirit.

On Christmas Day, everyone attends church. Then it's back home for an enormous dinner. Goose or venison is the main dish. The afternoon of Christmas day might be devoted to a family outing that includes ice-skating. During the holiday season, city authorities in many towns put up speakers at outdoor ice-skating rinks, where skaters glide over the ice to the tune of a Strauss waltz.

A Christmas market in Innsbruck

New Year's Eve is an outdoor event where people go to the town square to hear the church bells ring in the coming year. In Vienna, this means a trip to Saint Stephen's to enjoy its enormous bells. The plaza becomes so packed with people at midnight on New Year's Eve that you can do little more than walk in the direction the crowd is walking. Some revelers stay until dawn, singing songs and laughing. Everyone looks forward to the next Christmas season.

Freud and Psychoanalysis

Psychoanalysis is not a religion, but some people believe it serves as a replacement for religion in much of the modern world. Psychoanalysis is a form of therapy that helps people deal with fears, anxiety, and sadness. Those who practice the therapy believe that mental illnesses troubling an adult are rooted in disturbing childhood experiences. Under psychoanalysis, a person is encouraged to talk about past traumas and thereby overcome his or her problems. The psychoanalytic movement was largely invented in Austria, and it was fostered by the brilliant doctor Sigmund Freud.

Sigmund Freud in 1920

Freud was born on May 6, 1856, to a prosperous Jewish family in a region of Austria-Hungary that is now part of the Czech Republic. At the age of four, Freud moved with his family to Vienna, where his father was a wool merchant. Freud graduated from the University of Vienna in 1881. As a young doctor, he specialized in a malady that is now loosely called hysteria. Some patients suffering from this malady went blind or were paralyzed even though there seemed to be nothing wrong with them physically. Freud and a few other doctors argued that hysteria stemmed from mental disorders that affected the physical body. At first, Freud's ideas were rejected by the medical community.

Anna Freud

Anna Freud (1895–1982) was a world-famous doctor who treated mental illness in children. She was strongly influenced by the theories of her father, Sigmund Freud. Anna Freud believed that children go through certain precise stages of development, and that doctors should observe those stages when they treat disturbed children. Freud traveled with her father to London, England, after the Nazi takeover of Austria. In London, she established a clinic that dealt with the emotional problems of children.

Two early followers of Freud were Alfred Adler (1870–1937) and Carl Jung (1875–1961). Adler was an Austrian, and Jung was born in Switzerland. Adler and Jung held theories that differed slightly from Freud's, but all three doctors believed that childhood experiences were a powerful influence in molding the adult personality. Adler practiced in Vienna. In the early 1900s, Vienna was unchallenged as the world's leading center for the study of mental disorders.

Vienna's Monument to Freud

From 1891 through 1938, Sigmund Freud lived and saw patients in a Vienna apartment at Number 19 Berggasse Street. Freud urged his patients to relax by lying on a couch. To this day, many people consider a couch to be the symbol of psychiatry. The apartment on Berggasse still contains many of the Freud family's possessions. It is open to the public, and tourists come to see the items—including Freud's famous couch.

Living the Good Life

SOME OBSERVERS CLAIM AUSTRIANS ARE A "SHOWY" people. It is said that on Sundays, Austrians put on fancy clothes that cost more than they can afford and parade around their city streets to show off their finery. There is no way to confirm whether this charge is true, but no one denies that Austrians appreciate the best in clothes, arts, literature, food, and music. This hunger for the good life may stem from the days of empire, when the aristocrats could afford whatever pleasures they desired. Ever since then, common people have tried to imitate the opulent lifestyle enjoyed by the ruling class. Today, every citizen can seek out the pleasures once enjoyed only by royalty.

Art for the Ages

In 1822, the American writer Washington Irving visited Vienna and said it "is one of the most perplexing cities that I was ever in. . . . It has immense palaces, superb galleries of paintings, theaters. . . . In short everything that bears the stamp of luxury; for here is assembled all the wealth, fashion, and nobility of the Austrian Empire." The days of empire are long gone, but the exquisite collections of artworks that

Opposite: **Bicycling in the countryside**

Vienna's Museum of Fine Arts

thrilled Washington Irving remain. Today, the paintings and statues are housed in museums for the wonder and the enjoyment of all the people.

The art treasures of the Habsburg family are kept in Vienna's Kunsthistorisches Museum, also called the Museum of Fine Arts. This is truly one of the most splendid art museums in the world. Paintings and statues ranging from ancient Egyptian times to the twentieth century are displayed in its galleries. The popular picture gallery on the first floor is devoted to German, Dutch, and Flemish paintings. The works of Pieter Brueghel the Elder (1525?–1569), the great Flemish master, always attract the largest crowds. Brueghel had a particular genius for creating sweeping scenes that involve hundreds of people. Such a scene can be observed in *The Battle between Carnival and Lent* (1559). The Museum of Fine Arts cannot be seen in a single day. Many art lovers spend weeks studying the masterpieces housed there.

Expectation by Gustav Klimt

As a reward for his bravery in the war against the Turks in 1683, Prince Eugene of Savoy was granted permission to build his magnificent palace, the Belvedere, in Vienna. But the Habsburgs regarded Prince Eugene as a rival for their throne. After he died without heirs in 1736, the Habsburgs never again allowed any of their subjects to live in Belvedere. Today, the great palace is a museum that holds paintings of Austria's best twentieth-century artists such as Gustav Klimt, Egon Schiel, and Oskar Kokoschka.

The Splendor of Palaces

Austrian palaces are spectacles of history and architecture, and they often contain outstanding exhibits of art. For these reasons, a tour of Austrian palaces tops the lists of many tourists. Here are a few of them:

- *Schattenburg Castle* (Vorarlberg Province). Dating to the year 1200, this castle lies in the lovely town of Feldkirch. The castle now houses a Museum of Local History.

- *Ambras Castle* (Tyrol). Rising from a mountainside near Innsbruck, Ambras Castle features a collection of ancient swords and a fine gallery of paintings.

- *Orth Castle* (Upper Austria). Its lakeside location in the town of Gmunden makes a tour of this castle a scenic treat.

- *Herberstein Palace* (Styria). A splendid palace built in the baroque style, it houses a gallery of modern paintings.

- *Hochosterwitz Castle* (Carinthia). The Hochosterwitz (above) was used as a model by the Walt Disney artists who created the 1937 movie *Snow White and the Seven Dwarfs*. Built on an isolated mountain, it is one of Europe's most picturesque castles.

The Bride of the Wind
by Oskar Kokoschka

One of Austria's greatest painters of the twentieth century was Oskar Kokoschka (1886–1980). Kokoschka was famous for his portraits, which probed peoples' inner feelings. His wild brush strokes and use of color display a restless energy. In one famous painting, *The Bride of the Wind*, Kokoschka presents

The Golden Cabbage

Artists and architects tend to be a rebellious lot. In the late 1800s, a group of Vienna artists, headed by Gustav Klimt, grew disgusted with galleries that displayed only the paintings done in old-fashioned traditional styles. Klimt proclaimed, "The Arts lead us into the Kingdom of the Ideal." Led by Klimt, a group of artists created their own exhibition hall in Vienna. The structure, completed in 1898, was called the Secession Building. It featured a domed top made up of more than 3,000 cast-iron, gold-painted leaves. Today, the Secession Building is nicknamed "The Golden Cabbage."

two lovers swept up by wild winds in a stormy landscape. Kokoschka lived in Vienna in the 1930s. He criticized the policies of the Nazi Party, and, facing prison, he fled to London. He later lived in Switzerland.

Students of painting and sculpture study at Vienna's *Akademie der bildenden Künste* (Academy of Fine Arts). Founded in 1692, the academy has a gallery of paintings created by students and teachers over the ages. In the early 1900s, an aspiring artist named Adolf Hitler applied for admission at the Academy of Fine Arts. The young Hitler was devastated when a panel of teachers determined that his paintings displayed little promise and denied his application for admission. His failure in art led him to pursue a career in politics. Now the world wishes Hitler had lived as a little-talented but more-or-less harmless artist, instead of becoming the primary architect of World War II.

Literature

Austrians are a reading people. It is no wonder that Austrian literature has always been a powerful force in their society.

Studying in a Vienna park

In medieval times, Austrian and German literature and drama were intertwined. Minstrels and troubadours wearing colorful costumes traveled from town to town in Germany and Austria reciting poetry, singing songs, and staging plays. Such street entertainment is still common in Austrian cities. An epic poem called the *Nibelungenlied* (*The Song of the Nibelungs*), written by an unknown author around 1200, is considered to be the greatest work of Austrian literature in the Middle Ages. The poem told the story of revenge and intrigue in a king's court.

Franz Grillparzer (1791–1872) was one of Austria's greatest playwrights. He often set his stories about jealousy and love in historical times. In Grillparzer's play *The Golden Fleece*, figures of Greek mythology suffer human failures and everyday troubles. Ferdinand Raimund (1790–1836) and Johann Nepomuk Nestroy (1801–1862) wrote plays in Vienna that are still performed. Both Raimund and Nestroy favored comedies that included masked characters and bizarre situations.

A portrait of Franz Grillparzer by Moritz Michael Daffinger

Arnold Schnitzler (1862–1931), who was born in Vienna, was a doctor, a writer, and a friend of Sigmund Freud. In his plays and stories, Schnitzler concentrated on the psychological makeup of his characters. One of his best-loved plays is *Anatol*, which tells the adventures of a young man

The Burgtheater

You will often hear Viennese say, in excited voices, "We're going to the Burg tonight." They are referring to the Burgtheater, the center of Austria's dramatic scene. Standing in the heart of Vienna, the great theater was built between 1874 and 1888. Its inside ceilings are covered with paintings by the Austrian artists Franz Matsch and Gustav Klimt. It is a government-supported theater, and its selection of plays for the coming season is always the subject of intense debate. The Burgtheater was severely damaged during World War II, but the building has been lovingly restored.

in love. Vienna-born Hugo von Hofmannsthal (1874–1929) also penetrated the minds of his characters when writing plays. A music lover, Hofmannsthal worked with the German composer Richard Strauss and wrote the *librettos* (text) for many popular Strauss operas.

Rainer Maria Rilke (1875–1926) was born in Prague in the old Austro-Hungarian Empire and became a leading German-language poet. The poems in his *Book of Hours* tell of a soul seeking union with God. A restless spirit, Rilke spent much of his life wandering about Europe. Another writer born in Prague was Franz Kafka (1883–1924), who came from a German-speaking Jewish family. Kafka's novels are widely read in Austria and around the world even though they are often tales of despair featuring people who are consistently frustrated in reaching their goals.

One of the country's leading contemporary writers is Peter Handke, who was born 1942. Handke is a novelist with a strong social

Austrian writer Peter Handke

Austrian Films

Movies made in Austria are shown in Austria and Germany but are generally ignored outside the German-speaking world. Exceptions to this pattern are the films directed by Fritz Lang (1890–1976). Born in Vienna, Lang studied painting before taking up a career in the movies. Perhaps his most famous work is *Metropolis*, a silent movie that envisions a grim future in which machines have taken over the lives of human beings. Lang left Austria because he feared the growing power of the Nazi movement. He moved to the United States, where he directed many U.S. films including *Fury* (1936), the study of a lynch mob.

conscience. In 1999, he wrote an essay denouncing the war then raging in Yugoslavia. In the essay, Handke compared the entire earth to the unfortunate Yugoslav landscape. Austria's reading public will always be receptive to talented writers.

Music—The Austrian Triumph

Study Austria, and you are likely to conclude that there must be some musical magic carried in the winds that sweep the land. No other nation has produced so many geniuses whose tones and melodies have thrilled the world. Music is the proudest tradition of this proud country.

The modern music scene ranges from oom-pah-pah brass bands playing in village squares to the disco and jazz clubs of Vienna. Symphonic music, chamber music, and opera remain national favorites. Four major symphony orchestras perform in Vienna, and each province and most large towns also host orchestras. The waltz is heard everywhere.

The word *waltz* comes from a German term meaning "to turn." Its beat is simple—one, two, three; one, two, three. Light and airy, waltz music is so compelling that few can listen

Wolfgang Amadeus Mozart

Near Saint Stephen's Cathedral in Vienna, young men and women dressed in eighteenth-century costumes sell tickets to a Mozart concert. The ticket-sellers target tourists, telling them that this is a once-in-a-lifetime opportunity to see Mozart performed in the very room where the great master used to play and write music. Usually, all the tickets are sold in a matter of hours. Such is the worldwide appeal of Wolfgang Amadeus Mozart.

Born in Salzburg in 1756, Mozart was a child prodigy. He played the piano at age five and wrote original compositions at six. His father, a respected musician, took the boy on tours to European capitals. He once played before the Austrian Empress Maria Theresa at the Schönbrunn Palace, and at the conclusion of his performance, the six-year-old Mozart gave the empress a kiss. When he was in his twenties, Mozart moved to Vienna, where he concentrated on writing symphonies, chamber music, and opera. In all, he composed more than 600 works, including some of the most exquisite music ever written—the fairy-tale opera *The Magic Flute*, the powerful *Jupiter Symphony*, and beguiling serenades such as *A Little Night Music*. However, Mozart found it hard to make a living in

Vienna simply by writing music, and his finances were further complicated by a weakness for gambling. Mozart died in poverty in 1791 at age thirty-five and was buried in a pauper's grave at the Cemetery of Saint Mark in Vienna. His music will live forever.

and resist an urge to dance. Unchallenged as the Waltz King is Vienna-born Johann Strauss Jr. (1825–1899). Acting against his father's wishes, the young Strauss formed his own orchestra and wrote music. Vienna was one of the most romantic cities in the world at that time, and the Waltz King captured its spirit with wonderful pieces such as "On the Beautiful Blue Danube," "The Emperor Waltz," and "Tales from the Vienna Woods."

The music of Strauss and other waltz masters comes vibrantly alive in the gala balls held in Vienna. Balls are elegant dances where everyone wears striking clothes—tuxedos for the men and fancy gowns for the women. Such fashionable balls date back generations, to a time when Austrian army officers attended state parties decked out in dazzling uniforms. Balls are romantic affairs where hearts are won and promises of marriage are exchanged. Yet a long-standing tradition says that a gentleman attending a ball may kiss his lady guest only

Vienna's Opera Ball in 1998

The Staatsoper

Seeing a performance at the *Staatsoper* (State Opera House) is a highlight of any trip to Vienna. Among music-loving Austrians, the building is looked upon as a shrine. There is, however, a touch of tragedy about the structure. As the story goes, when the Staatsoper was completed in 1869, Emperor Franz Josef took a brief inspection tour. He complained, mildly, that the audience in certain seats had a poor view of the stage. The building's two principal architects were so devastated by the criticism that one promptly killed himself and the other soon died of grief. Franz Josef, who took pride in his gentle manners, never again said a negative word about an Austrian building for fear of offending the architects.

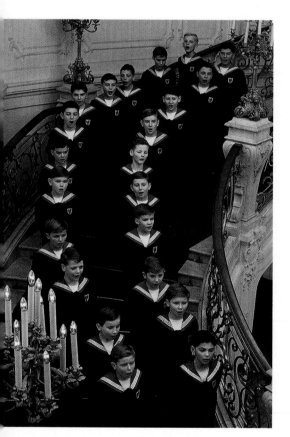

One of the four groups of the Vienna Boys' Choir

on the hand. All classes of Viennese society rent huge dance halls and hold balls. These include a Pastry Cooks' Ball, a Florists' Ball, a Police Ball, and a Coffee Brewers' Ball. In all, about 300 balls are held in Vienna during January and February. Tickets to the Opera Ball are the most expensive and sought after. The Opera Ball is held in Vienna's ornate Opera House, where the seats are removed so that hundreds of dancers can waltz through the night.

One of the country's most famous musical institutions is the Vienna Boys' Choir. Established as a church choir in 1498, this world-renowned singing group has entertained audiences for 500 years. Great composers such as Josef Haydn and Franz Schubert once sang in the choir. Today, the choir consists of eighty-eight boys, divided into four groups. Their ages range from eleven to thirteen. A group of judges selects the boys based on the sweetness of their voices and their knowledge of music. Once chosen, the choirboys travel the world,

The Great Musical Debut

Lovers of classical music consider Ludwig van Beethoven's Ninth Symphony, called the *Choral Symphony*, to be the most uplifting and spiritual piece ever written. The mood of this symphony ranges from darkness to light, from a solemn tone to a glorious note of triumph. Beethoven based the last movement on the German poet Friedrich von Schiller's verse "Ode to Joy." Its message is captured wonderfully in the words "All men will be brothers."

The Ninth Symphony was first performed in Vienna on May 7, 1824. Reports say the audience was silent and that many people left before the magnificent last movement was completed. Beethoven was standing on the stage during the concert, but he heard nothing because by this time he was almost completely deaf. Shortly after its debut, the Ninth Symphony caught fire with European audiences and was heralded as perhaps the greatest musical work ever composed.

singing before packed houses. At home, they live in a special dormitory at Vienna's Augarten Palace, and continue their education despite their globe-trotting tours. To become a Vienna choirboy is the burning ambition of thousands of young Austrian singers.

Sports

An American visiting Vienna could not help but notice the people's eating habits. Day after day, they consumed pastries smothered with whipped cream. Yet few people he saw on the streets had that roly-poly look so common in the United States. Finally, the American asked a waitress why it was that the Viennese, given their choice of food, did not get fat. The waitress smiled and said, "Because we like too much the skiing."

Sports are a passion in Austria. In the summer months, people hike, bicycle, swim, and go on mountain-climbing parties. The favorite team sport is soccer. Hotly contested soccer

Hermann Maier at the finish line of the Men's Downhill race at the 1999 World Alpine Ski Championships

matches are held at the huge *Praterstadion*, a stadium in Vienna's world-famous Prater Park. Winter sports include skiing, ice-skating, bobsledding, ice hockey, and tobogganing. Many children learn to ski at age five or six. Skier Hermann Maier became a national hero when he won two gold medals in the 1998 Winter Olympics in Nagano, Japan.

Austrians are enchanted with equestrian sports. Horses and their riders march proudly in military parades. Polo is the preferred sport for the well-to-do. Horse-drawn carriages, called *Fiakers*, are a favorite way to get around Vienna. Racing at the *Freudenau*, a 100-year-old racetrack in Vienna, is a society event. Viennese put on their best clothes and take opera glasses to the Freudenau to cheer on their favorite horse.

The country's most famous horses perform at the *Spanische Reitschule* (Spanish Riding School) in Vienna. The Spanish Riding School has enchanted spectators for more than 300 years. In an amazing ballet, horses prance in precise weaving formations to the strains of baroque music. The horses are white Lipizzaners, a breed that originated in Spain. Their riders are carefully selected and highly skilled. Centuries ago, horses similar to these Lipizzaners led Austrian cavalry soldiers into battle. Now, horses and riders present eighty-minute

shows to thrilled audiences. There's only one problem: The Spanish Riding School is such a popular attraction that tickets to the shows must be ordered months in advance.

A performance at the
Spanish Riding School

Athlete Turned Hollywood Star

Arnold Schwarzenegger (far right) was born in Graz in 1947. As a boy, he was an outstanding athlete, excelling in swimming. He became interested in bodybuilding and won several awards, including Mr. Universe. He next turned his muscleman image to Hollywood. Schwarzenegger debuted in what critics agreed was a perfectly awful movie—*Hercules in New York*. He went on to star in action movies, including the popular *Terminator* science-fiction adventures, and then appeared in lighthearted—even silly—comedies such as *Kindergarten Cop* and *Jingle All the Way*.

Everyday Life in a Storybook Land

L IVING IN AUSTRIA IS LIKE LIVING IN A MUSEUM. THERE are centuries-old buildings and outstanding works of art everywhere. But within this atmosphere, people still go to work, go to school, fall in love, and get married. These events happen here just as they do anywhere in the world. But in Austria the past is always present, and the shadow of history is cast over all.

Opposite: **Houses in a suburb of Vienna**

A girl in traditional Austrian costume

Rural Life

In the past, Austrians were a farming people, raising wheat and barley on level land and tending cattle on the hilly slopes. Today, the vast majority of Austrians live in cities and towns. Farming has become mechanized, and fewer than 2 percent of the people work on the land now. Still, it is primarily the rural people who keep old traditions alive through their fairs and festivals.

On holidays, farm families dig into their chests to bring out special costumes that depict typical farm dress of a century ago. Men wear lederhosen—short leather pants with straps over the shoulders. Women and girls put on a dirndl—a dress and hat outfit that blazes with color. Traditionally adorned, the people entertain fellow villagers

On holidays, people dress up in traditional clothes and entertain with folk dancing.

and tourists with singing and folk dancing. Country weddings are usually held outdoors in the summer months. These outdoor weddings call for a lively *Schuhplatter*—a foot-stamping dance in which men slap their knees and women spin wildly as a brass band plays polka music.

Dairy farmers in parts of Austria dress up their cows as a way of telling their neighbors they have had a good harvest. When harvest time is over, they make headdresses of flowers and put them on their cows. With the cows' heads properly garlanded, the farmers parade their herds down country roads for everyone to see.

Cows wearing headdresses of flowers are paraded down country roads to signify a good harvest.

Just outside Vienna, farmers grow grapes that they make into wine. The wine is served in special taverns called *Heurigen*. The word *Heurigen* means "this year's," and it refers to the new wine grown in a nearby vineyard and made in the tavern's kitchen. Tavern guests eat and drink while sitting at long pine picnic tables next to the wine barrels. They listen to the music of an accordion and a singer provided by the establishment. The Heurigens serve enormous buffet meals of salads, sausages, and fruit. Heurigens have operated near Vienna for hundreds of years. Following an ancient tradition, the tavern owner places a bunch of pine twigs on a metal bar over the door to indicate that the establishment is open and the new wine is ready to be served.

The Pleasures of Food

Few things are more important to the Austrian way of life than good food. It is often said that some people eat to live while others live to eat. Austrians count themselves in the latter category. With a population of more than 8 million, Austria supports an amazing 50,000 restaurants.

The Revival of Yodeling

The art of yodeling was born in the mountains of Switzerland and Austria. Years ago, yodelers were the "telephones" that allowed isolated mountain villages to communicate with one another. Romantics claim that yodeling was also the secret language of young men and their sweethearts who lived in neighboring towns.

Some time ago, yodeling lost favor with young people, but the 1990s saw a revival of the old custom. Hermann Haertel, a professional yodeler, is not surprised. "Yodeling is the music of the mountains," says Haertel. "It is a powerful cry that comes from the soul, and once you start, it becomes addictive."

A restaurant on Vienna's Fleischmarkt street has been a public eating house since the 1500s. Over the centuries, its owners have encouraged famous patrons to sign the walls. The signatures are still there, and waiters proudly point them out. Signers include Beethoven, Mozart, the Strausses (father and son), Ferdinand von Zeppelin (the inventor of lighter-than-air vehicles), and the American writer Mark Twain.

The Austrian favorite *Weiner schnitzel* (a pork or veal cutlet that is breaded and fried) is a mainstay of menus throughout the country. Other meat dishes include *Backhendl* (fried chicken), *Zwiebelrostbraten* (roast beef smothered in fried onions), and *Tafelspitz* (boiled beef in horseradish sauce). Meat is served with potatoes or dumplings and at least one vegetable. Red cabbage and sauerkraut—an old German standby—are favorite vegetable dishes.

Weiner schnitzel with red cabbage is a favorite Austrian dish.

The Eastern European influence over Austrian cuisine is seen in the delicious stew called *Gulasch* (goulash), which is served at many restaurants. Street vendors dish out food from pushcarts and tiny stands. At the *Wurstelstand* (sausage stand), hot dog–like sausages are served on buns. Regional cooking is an exciting treat for vacationers. The province of Carinthia produces *Käsnudl*, a pasta creation similar to ravioli with a cheese filling. Tyrol is famous for *Tiroler Knödel*, dumplings made with small pieces of ham. Austrian provinces have their own personalities, which emerge gloriously in regional cooking.

Fish is popular, especially in rural areas where mountain streams run pure. *Forelle* (trout) and *Hecht* (a native pike) are staples in country inns and restaurants. Health-conscious tourists and Austrians alike enjoy the many vegetarian establishments that have popped up in recent years. Fruits and vegetables served in such restaurants are grown locally and always fresh.

An estimated 700 Chinese restaurants are now operating in Austria, along with a large number of Indian, Thai, and Japanese places. Of course, you can always eat under the Golden Arches. McDonald's has become popular with young people who enjoy meal-in-a-minute lunches.

Coffeehouses, which serve coffee, tea, and pastries, are beloved in Vienna. They provide a place for friends to meet and discuss sports or politics. Young lovers begin their dates at the neighborhood coffeehouse. Moreover, the coffeehouses are a symbol of an elegant, unhurried way of life. Sipping coffee slowly is the custom in such places. Many a *Kaffeehaus*

Coffee—The Gift of War

In wartime, even the bitterest of enemies manage to exchange goods. During the 1600s, the Austrians and the Turks fought a bloody series of wars. A legend says that in the 1683 siege of Vienna, the Viennese people smelled an enticing aroma wafting over the Turkish lines every morning. A bold Viennese soldier ventured out and traded with the Turks for a bag of the strange black beans that produced the aroma. It marked a historic moment—the day Vienna discovered coffee. Is the legend true? No one knows for sure, but it is certain the Viennese went daffy over coffee. Coffeehouses became the rage in the Austrian capital.

provides a rack of newspapers for its customers. Others encourage people to play chess. Customers establish long-term relationships with their favorite coffeehouse and know the staff and their families. Some customers even get their mail at their coffeehouse. However, the furious pace of modern life is

A window full of pastries at Demel's Coffeehouse

eroding the coffeehouse tradition. In the early 1900s, some 400 coffeehouses served Vienna. Today, only a few hundred of the old establishments remain.

Pastry is the pride of Austria. Pastry cooks go to school for three years before they can even start out as apprentices. Most cafes and coffeehouses display tortes and cakes in a glass case, and customers simply point to the scrumptious treat they desire. A few examples of these treats are *Apfelstrudel* (raisins and apples wrapped in a pastry envelope); *Linzertorte* (made with jam and almond-flavored dough); *Dobostorte* (a Hungarian specialty with chocolate icing); and *Sachertorte*, a Viennese creation, and perhaps the most famous pastry in the world.

Participating in sports helps to keep Austrians fit despite their love of rich food. Today, there is a tendency among many Austrians, especially the young, to cut back on creamy desserts and fatty meats. Yet many Austrians refuse to give up their traditional high-fat foods. Such stout, pot-bellied people are called *Wurstfressers* (sausage-gobblers). Food is life in Austria. Even the most refined gourmets from around the world consider Austria to be the king of cuisine.

City Life

The streets of Vienna burst into life early each day as people rush to work and children go to school. Most workers take the streetcar, the subway, or the bus to their jobs. Children either walk to school or take regular public transportation. Few special school buses operate in Vienna. Despite the availability of mass transit, many people drive cars to work, so traffic jams in the Austrian capital can be ferocious.

Shops in Vienna and other cities open about nine in the morning. Food shopping in urban Austria is a different experience from that in the United States. People go to a meat market to buy meat, a fish market for fish, and a produce store

Noisy Neighbor

The city of Vienna publishes guidebooks so that tourists can see where famous residents such as Mozart and Freud once lived. Beethoven is listed in these books, but he lived in some forty different apartments during his years in Vienna. He was a grumpy man and frequently argued with neighbors and landlords. Plus, he was profoundly deaf in later life and had to bang on his piano in order to hear notes. So Beethoven—whose music is so sweet and spiritual—was forced to move often.

for fruits and vegetables. In some towns, pastry shops sell only cakes and tortes, and bread shops sell only bread and rolls. For Austrians, shopping is an excuse to chat and exchange gossip with their neighbors. However, customs change even in a time-honored country such as Austria. More and more U.S.-style supermarkets are opening. These large stores, surrounded by a parking lot, offer all kinds of food under one roof.

Vienna is filled with colorful attractions, such as the Hundred Waters House shown here.

Everyday Life in a Storybook Land   **123**

When visiting Vienna, hop on the number-one streetcar to take the historic ride of your life. That streetcar runs along *Ringstrasse* (Ring Street)—a U-shaped boulevard that begins and ends at the Danube Canal and encompasses the city's historic heart. In olden times, the city walls that fended off the Turks and other invading armies stood on Ring Street, but the walls were torn down in the 1850s to create the semicircular boulevard. From the streetcar window, you will see many of Vienna's outstanding buildings: the State Opera, the Burgtheater, and Hofburg Palace, to name a few. The trip around Ring Street takes about twenty minutes. Happy riding!

Restaurants pick up business about noon. In fact, many restaurants do not open for breakfast, which is usually a light meal in Austria. Children pour out of school about three in the afternoon, and the sidewalks are noisy again. Scores of kids head to city parks to play pick-up soccer games or race over the walkways on skateboards. Parks are the lungs of urban Austria. They are a refuge where anyone can sit or stroll among greenery and escape the tension of the big city. Parks throughout the nation are kept clean and safe.

The largest park, and one of the greatest city parks in the world, is Vienna's Prater Park. Sprawling over 3,200 acres (1,295 hectares), the Prater—once a private hunting ground for royalty—has been a public park for more than 200 years. One portion of the Prater is an amusement park complete with merry-go-rounds, roller coasters, and other attractions. A city landmark is Prater Park's 209-foot (63.7-m)-tall Ferris wheel, which was erected in 1897. Beyond the amusement park are bicycle paths and trails where people take long, thoughtful walks. It is impossible to imagine Vienna without the wonderful Prater Park.

Opposite: **Prater Park's famous 209-foot-tall Ferris wheel**

In late afternoon, Vienna's street entertainers appear. The best place to catch their acts is on the pedestrian-only streets that radiate out from Saint Stephen's Cathedral. You'll see jugglers, tumblers, mimes, magicians, and comics. All wear colorful costumes and attract amused bystanders. Crowds gather in front of a thin young man who works a puppet that is an amazing Elvis Presley look-alike. An extraordinarily beautiful young woman wears a Roman toga and stands still, imitating a statue. The street entertainment is free—so to speak. All the performers have a basket or a hat standing near their act, and they hope for contributions from generous patrons.

At seven o'clock, nightlife begins in the city. The quality of nightlife varies from city to city and town to town. Theaters open. Restaurants and hotel dance halls come alive with the music of Strauss. Concerts are always performed in this most musical of all nations. It is estimated that at least one Mozart concert is put on somewhere in Austria every night of the year. In Vienna, the amusement park at the Prater throbs with laughter and people swooning on the high rides. Finally, long after midnight, the city streets fall silent as the nation sleeps. Dawn will bring a new day to the storybook land of Austria.

An evening view over the city of Salzburg

Timeline

Austrian History

The Roman Empire controls Austria south of the Danube.	15 B.C.
Northern tribes begin invading Austria, weakening Roman control.	A.D. 166
Austria comes under the rule of Holy Roman emperor Otto I of Germany.	955
Control of northeastern Austria is given to Leopold I of the Badenburg family.	976
A member of the Habsburg family, Holy Roman emperor Rudolf I, begins acquiring Austrian lands.	1278
The Habsburg Maximilian I marries his son to the daughter of a Spanish king, extending Habsburg influence into Spain.	1496
The Thirty Years' War begins when many Austrians reject the Catholic Church, choosing Protestantism.	1618
The Peace of Westphalia ends the Thirty Years' War, allowing Habsburg leaders to impose Catholicism on their subjects.	1648
With the help of Polish and German soldiers, invading Ottomans are repelled outside Vienna.	1683

World History

2500 B.C.	Egyptians build the Pyramids and Sphinx in Giza.
563 B.C.	Buddha is born in India.
A.D. 313	The Roman emperor Constantine recognizes Christianity.
610	The prophet Muhammad begins preaching a new religion called Islam.
1054	The Eastern (Orthodox) and Western (Roman) Churches break apart.
1066	William the Conqueror defeats the English in the Battle of Hastings.
1095	Pope Urban II proclaims the First Crusade.
1215	King John seals the Magna Carta.
1300s	The Renaissance begins in Italy.
1347	The Black Death sweeps through Europe.
1453	Ottoman Turks capture Constantinople, conquering the Byzantine Empire.
1492	Columbus arrives in North America.
1500s	The Reformation leads to the birth of Protestantism.

Austrian History

Charles VI declares the Pragmatic Sanction, allowing his daughter Maria Theresa to inherit the throne.	1713
The War of the Austrian Succession is fought as European neighbors resist Maria Theresa's rule.	1740–1748
The Holy Roman Empire ends after Napoléon I conquers much of the empire.	1806
Prince Klemens von Metternich represents the Austrian Empire at the Congress of Vienna, ushering in a temporary peace.	1814–1815
The Dual Monarchy of Austria-Hungary is declared, with Austrians swearing allegiance to one monarch who is both emperor of Austria and king of Hungary.	1867
Archduke Franz Ferdinand is assassinated; Austria-Hungary declares war on Serbia, beginning World War I.	1914
World War I ends in defeat for Austria and the Central Powers; the last Habsburg emperor is overthrown and Austria emerges as a republic.	1918
A new Constitution establishes a parliamentary democracy.	1920
German troops march into Austria; Hitler announces the Anschluss (union) of Austria and Germany.	1938
World War II ends; Austria is occupied by the Allies.	1945
Allied forces are withdrawn; Austria declares permanent neutrality in all foreign affairs and joins the United Nations.	1955
Austria hosts the Strategic Arms Limitation Talks (SALT), designed to limit weapons of mass destruction.	1969
Innsbruck hosts the Winter Olympic Games.	1976
Kurt Waldheim is elected president despite allegations of links to Nazi war crimes.	1986
Austria becomes a member of the European Union.	1995

World History

1776	The Declaration of Independence is signed.
1789	The French Revolution begins.
1865	The American Civil War ends.
1914	World War I breaks out.
1917	The Bolshevik Revolution brings Communism to Russia.
1929	Worldwide economic depression begins.
1939	World War II begins, following the German invasion of Poland.
1957	The Vietnam War starts.
1989	The Berlin Wall is torn down, as Communism crumbles in Eastern Europe.
1996	Bill Clinton is reelected U.S. president.

Fast Facts

Official name: Republic of Austria (*Republik Österreich*)

Capital: Vienna

Official language: German

Hikers in Tyrol

Austrian flag

A lakeside village

Official religion:	None
Year of founding:	1918 as a republic; reestablished 1945
National anthem:	*"Land der Berge, Land am Strome"* ("Land of Mountains, Land of Rivers")
Government:	Federal republic
Chief of state:	President
Head of government:	Chancellor
Area and dimensions:	32,375 square miles (83,845 square km); 355 miles (571 km) east to west, 180 miles (290 km) north to south
Latitude and longitude of geographic center:	47° 20' North, 13° 20' East
Land borders:	Germany and the Czech Republic on the north; Slovakia and Hungary on the east; Slovenia and Italy on the south; Liechtenstein and Switzerland on the west.
Highest elevation:	Grossglockner, 12,457 feet (3,797 m) above sea level
Lowest elevation:	Neusiedler Lake, 377 feet (115 m) below sea level
Average temperature extremes:	27°F (–3°C) in January; 67°F (19°C) in July
Average annual precipitation:	25 inches (64 cm)
National population (1999 est.):	8,139,299

Graz

Population of largest cities (1991 est.):

Vienna	1,539,848
Graz	232,150
Linz	203,000
Salzburg	144,000
Innsbruck	115,000

Famous landmarks:

▶ *The Burgtheater* (Vienna)

▶ *Kunsthistorisches Museum* (Vienna); also called the Museum of Fine Arts

▶ *Palaces and castles:*
Ambras Castle (Tyrol);
Herberstein Palace (Styria);
Hochosterwitz Castle (Carinthia);
Orth Castle (Upper Austria); and
Schattenburg Castle (Feldkirch, in Vorarlberg Province)

▶ *The Spanish Riding School* (Vienna)

▶ *The Staatsoper (State Opera House)* (Vienna)

Industry: Construction, machinery, vehicles and parts, food, chemicals, lumber and wood processing, paper and paperboard, communications equipment, and tourism

Currency: Austrian schilling. Early 2000 exchange rate: U.S.$1 = 13.86 Austrian schillings. In 1999, Austria began replacing the local currency with the euro, a common European currency. The euro will replace the Austrian schilling for all transactions in 2002.

System of weights and measures: Metric system

Currency

A Viennese flea market

Sigmund Freud

Literacy:	Virtually 100 percent	
Common German words and phrases:	*Bitte*	Please
	Danke.	Thank you.
	Bitte sehr.	You're welcome.
	Guten Abend.	Good evening.
	Hier, da	Here, there
	Wieviel?	How much?
	Auf Wiedersehen.	Good-bye.
Famous people:	Alfred Adler *Psychoanalyst*	(1870–1937)
	Ludwig van Beethoven *Composer*	(1770–1827)
	Anna Freud *Child psychoanalyst*	(1895–1982)
	Sigmund Freud *Founder of psychoanalysis*	(1856–1939)
	Franz Joseph Haydn *Composer*	(1732–1809)
	Gregor Johann Mendel *Monk and scientist*	(1822–1884)
	Wolfgang Amadeus Mozart *Composer*	(1756–1791)
	Rainer Maria Rilke *Poet*	(1875–1926)
	Franz Peter Schubert *Composer*	(1797–1828)
	Arnold Schwarzenegger *Athlete and movie star*	(1947–)
	Johann Strauss Sr. *Composer*	(1804–1849)
	Johann Strauss Jr. *Composer*	(1825–1899)

To Find Out More

Nonfiction

▶ Blakely, Roger K. *Wolfgang Amadeus Mozart*. San Diego: Lucent Books, 1991.

▶ Hughes, Helga. *Cooking the Austrian Way*. Minneapolis: Lerner Publications, 1990.

▶ Lerner Geography Staff. *Austria in Pictures*. Easy Menu Ethnic Cookbook Series. Minneapolis: Lerner Publications, 1991.

▶ Lewis, Jerry. *Ludwig von Beethoven: The Composer Who Continued to Write Music after He Became Deaf*. New York: Chelsea House, 1995.

▶ McLenighan, Valjean. *Christmas in Austria*. Chicago: World Book Press, 1982.

▶ Muckenhoupt, Margaret. *Sigmund Freud: Explorer of the Unconscious*. New York: Oxford University Press, 1997.

▶ Orgel, Doris. *The Devil in Vienna*. New York: Puffin Books, 1988. A work of fiction about the friendship between a Jewish girl and the daughter of a Nazi in Vienna in 1938.

▶ Sheehan, Sean. *Cultures of the World: Austria*. New York: Marshall Cavendish, 1992.

▶ Stein, R. Conrad. *Vienna*. Cities of the World. Danbury, Conn.: Children's Press, 1998.

▶ Thompson, Wendy. *Joseph Haydn*. Minneapolis: Lerner Publications, 1991.

▶ Van der Linde, Laurel. *The White Stallions: The Story of the Dancing Horses of Lipizza*. New York: New Discovery Books, 1994.

Websites

▶ **Austria Culture Net**
http://www.austriaculture.net
Presented by the Austrian Cultural Institute and Communication House International, Inc., this site offers information on cultural events, science and education, news and more; includes links.

▶ **Austrian Press and Information Service**
http://www.austria.org
Print, audio, and television news from Austria, plus tourist information, video tours, and more.

Embassies and Organizations

▶ **Austrian Cultural Institute**
950 Third Avenue, 20th floor
New York, NY 10022
(212) 759-5165
http://www.austriaculture.net

▶ **Austrian Embassy**
3524 International Court, N.W.
Washington, DC 20008
(202) 895-6700

Index

Page numbers in *italics* indicate illustrations.

Meet the Author

R. Conrad Stein was born and grew up in Chicago. After serving in the U.S. Marines, he attended the University of Illinois and graduated with a degree in history. He is now a full-time writer of books for young readers. Over the years he has published more than 100 titles. Mr. Stein lives in Chicago with his wife, Deborah Kent, who also writes books for young readers, and their daughter, Janna.

Traveling and visiting foreign countries are Mr. Stein's passions. He has toured all the major countries of Europe, including Austria. Another of Mr. Stein's passions is classical music. He adores the works of the masters—Mozart, Beethoven, Haydn, Mahler, and Bach. This love of music has endeared the city of Vienna to him. He will never forget a thrilling performance of Mozart's opera *The Magic Flute* that he attended with his wife in Vienna's Opera House.

To prepare for this book, Mr. Stein read a half-dozen or more books on Austria, he spoke to Austrian government officials, and he listened to the music of Mozart, Haydn, and others. The music part of his research was a labor of love.

Photo Credits